STUFFED SPUDS:

100 Meals in a Potato

JEANNE JONES

M. EVANS AND COMPANY, INC.
NEW YORK

TO DICK DUFFY

My favorite Irishman, whose ancestors made this book possible by bringing potatoes to this country

IN GRATEFUL ACKNOWLEDGMENT:

Grace Bostic for recipe preparation and testing
Viola Stroup for technical and editorial assistance

M. Evans and Company, Inc.
216 East 49 Street
New York, New York 10017

Manufactured in the United States of America

CONTENTS

INTRODUCTION

The potato is certainly the most widely used vegetable in the Western world and is often called the world's most important vegetable. The plant probably originated in the Andes, where it was cultivated by the Incas in pre-Columbian times. The Spanish conquistadores discovered the *papa*, which they called *patatas* and shipped back to Spain as ship's stores. The potato is considered by many to have been a more valuable find for the world than all of the silver in Peru.

Ironically, the potato of South America took almost two centuries to reach North America and arrived by a circuitous route—from Spain to Italy to Northern Europe to Bermuda to the Virginia colonies in 1621. However, the real importance of potato growing did not start until the Irish immigrants brought them to Londonderry, New Hampshire, in 1719.

Potatoes have also had a great impact on history. White potatoes became the major food source in Ireland in the nineteenth century and are therefore often called Irish potatoes to distinguish them from sweet potatoes. In the potato blight in 1845, all of the potato plants all over Ireland turned black in the space of just a few weeks, and over a million Irish starved. The disease quickly spread to Europe. The Great Potato Famine greatly altered the population of the

United States, bringing thousands of Irish, Germans and Poles to our shores.

Potato is the common name for a perennial plant (*Solanum tuberosum*) of the family Solanaceae (nightshade family). It has a swollen underground stem or tuber. It grows best in a cool, moist climate. Most potatoes in the United States are now grown in Idaho, Washington, or Maine, although some are grown in all states.

Chemical analysis of the potato shows it to be high in potassium, phosphorus and iron. It is also a good source of vitamin C and calcium. Most of the minerals and protein are concentrated in a thin layer beneath the skin.

In today's diet-conscious society, potatoes are often regarded as "fattening," but they are not. One medium-size potato contains between 70 and 100 calories, less than the average serving of cottage cheese and fruit. However, the butter, sour cream, crumbled bacon and other popular high-fat toppings are "fattening" whether served on a potato or by themselves. In fact potatoes are an ideal diet food because they are approximately 75% water and therefore very filling. Because they are also high in dietary fiber you are not apt to be hungry again for a long time.

The new wave of stuffed spud restaurants both in this country and in Europe prompted me to write this cookbook. A meal in a potato can be as simple or as elaborate as you wish. It can be the most economical approach to meal planning available or very expensive, depending on the ingredients you choose to put in it. A stuffed spud can also be a dieter's dream—very low in calories and very high in nutrition—or it can be a total debauchery.

The recipes in this book run the gamut of all categories. Read through the book, make your own choices and then your shopping list. Start having fun stuffing spuds!

HELPFUL HINTS

The potatoes recommended for baking are either the russets or the all-purpose potatoes found in your market. The term "Idaho" is reserved for russets grown in Idaho. The all-purpose potato resembles the russet in shape but has a thinner skin.

The recipes call for two potatoes, which will give you two servings. You can halve, double, or triple the recipes as needed. Although I used three-quarter-pound potatoes for developing the recipes, you can use half-pound potatoes. If smaller potatoes are used, you can use three instead of two.

When you cut the tops from baked potatoes, store these tops in a tightly sealed container in the freezer. Then when you want deep-fried potato skins you have them all ready to use. Also try brushing them with butter or corn-oil margarine and putting them under the broiler until lightly browned and crisp. Serve broiled potato skins instead of toast, or as cocktail food with a dip, or chop them up and use them as croutons in soups and salads.

Although all recipes are for two potatoes, in a few recipes you only use the pulp from one potato. Store the unused pulp from the other potato in a tightly sealed container in the freezer to use later for mashed potatoes, potato pancakes, au gratin or cottage-fried potatoes.

11

In a few of the recipes you will have more filling than will fit into the potato shells, even by heaping it up. The leftover filling makes a good filling for omelets or can be stored in the freezer for use as a vegetable side dish at another meal.

Almost all of the stuffed spuds to be served hot can be prepared ahead of time and then reheated just before serving. When reheating them, put them in a 350°F. oven for 15 to 20 minutes. When making them ahead of time, do not garnish until after they have been reheated. Also, many of them are delicious cold and make wonderful school, work or picnic lunches.

I have read in many books that you cannot successfully freeze potatoes; however I have found this not to be true. In testing these recipes, we have frozen all of them and find that the only recipes which cannot be frozen successfully are the salad-type recipes containing fresh vegetables such as tomatoes, lettuce and cabbage. If you wish to freeze a salad-type recipe, do not add the shredded lettuce, cabbage, tomatoes, etc., until after the potato has thawed and you are ready to serve it. You will find that the reheated frozen stuffed spuds, whether taken directly from the freezer and reheated in a microwave oven for immediate serving, or thawed to room temperature and reheated in a conventional oven, are very good, perhaps not quite as good as they would have been before freezing, but certainly as good as the commercial TV dinners available at high prices in grocery stores. Create your own TV dinners; clean out the refrigerator and stuff some spuds, whether you're going to be home to eat them or not. Freeze them for future meals.

BASIC RECIPES
&
INGREDIENTS

Baked Potatoes

The following method is best for preparing potatoes for stuffing.

2 large baking potatoes

1. Preheat the oven to 400°F. Wash the potatoes well and dry thoroughly. Pierce with the tines of a fork to keep the skins from bursting.

2. Bake for 1 hour.

3. Remove potatoes from the oven and allow to cool until comfortable to the touch.

If you rub potatoes with oil or butter or wrap them in foil, you soften the skins in the process. You want as tough-textured a potato shell as possible so it can be stuffed without tearing. I used ¾-pound potatoes for developing and testing the recipes in this book.

I am also including two other interesting methods of preparation for baked potatoes which you may want to try.

Overbaked Potatoes

Recently I was telling James Beard about my upcoming stuffed spud book. He asked me if I had ever eaten a potato baked at 450°F. for 2 hours. I thought I had misunderstood him and asked again how long and at what temperature. He assured me that it was a perfectly wonderful way to serve a potato, unusual and delicious. He likes it served only with freshly ground black pepper. You may enjoy it in the James Beard style or you may prefer the more classic accompaniments, butter and salt. The potato itself has a very thick crunchy outer shell, almost like a pastry crust. The inside has a rich, buttery consistency, which in my opinion really does not need butter or sour cream. I like it with the fresh pepper and a little cottage cheese.

2 large baking potatoes

1. Preheat the oven to 450°F. Wash the potatoes well and dry thoroughly. Pierce them several times with the tines of a fork.

2. Place potatoes on the center rack of the preheated 450°F. oven and bake for 2 hours.

3. Remove potatoes from the oven and cut lengthwise and then across the middle, almost through them. The shells will be very crisp and thick and will not squeeze easily. Open the potatoes and mash the inside pulp as best you can with a fork.

Lined Potato "Bowls"

These lined potato "bowls" may be filled with any ingredients of your choice. They are convenient for serving leftovers of any type, such as chopped fish, poultry or meat, cooked vegetables, even soups and salads.

2 baked potatoes
2 tablespoons butter or corn-oil margarine
¼ cup cream or milk
Salt
Freshly ground white or black pepper as desired

1. Cut a thin slice from the top of each potato. Remove the pulp from the potatoes, being careful not to tear the shells. Place the potato pulp in a mixing bowl and mash. Set the shells aside.

2. Add butter or margarine, cream or milk, and seasoning to taste to the potatoes and mix thoroughly. Press through a sieve. Spoon the purée into the baked potato shells, pressing the mixture evenly over the entire inner surfaces with the back of a spoon.

Chicken Stock

3 pounds chicken parts (wings, backs, necks)
1 whole stewing chicken (optional)
2 carrots, scraped and cut into pieces
3 onions, cut into quarters
5 garlic cloves
2 parsley sprigs
2 bay leaves
1 teaspoon dried basil
¼ teaspoon peppercorns
Distilled water

1. Put the chicken parts (and the whole chicken if you want to cook one in addition to making stock) and all other ingredients in a large pot or soup kettle. Add cold distilled water to cover by 1 inch. Slowly bring to a boil.

2. Cover, leaving lid ajar about 1 inch to allow steam to escape. Simmer very slowly for 3 hours, until the whole chicken is tender.

3. Remove whole chicken and continue to simmer stock with chicken parts for 3 to 4 hours.

4. Cool stock to room temperature and put in the refrigerator, uncovered, overnight.

5. When the fat has hardened on the surface of the stock, remove it. Warm the defatted stock until it becomes liquid.

6. Strain the liquid and taste. If the flavor of the stock is too weak, boil it down to evaporate more of the liquid and concentrate its strength.

7. Store the stock in the freezer in the size container you will use most often. You can then take the stock directly from the freezer and melt it whenever you need it.

Makes about 2½ quarts (10 cups) stock.

Beef Stock

4 pounds beef or veal bones
3 large onions, cut into quarters
2 carrots, scraped and sliced
6 garlic cloves
4 parsley sprigs
2 whole cloves
1 teaspoon celery seeds
1 teaspoon dried thyme
1 teaspoon dried marjoram
2 bay leaves
¼ teaspoon peppercorns
1½ cups tomato juice (one 12-ounce can)
Defatted beef drippings (optional)
Distilled water

1. Preheat the oven to 400°F. Brown the bones in a roasting pan for 30 minutes.

2. Add the onions, carrots and garlic and brown together for another 30 minutes, or until ingredients are a rich, deep brown in color.

3. Put the browned meat and vegetables in a large pot or soup kettle with the remaining ingredients.

4. Add cold distilled water to cover by 1 inch. Bring to a boil, then reduce heat and simmer for 5 minutes; remove any scum that forms on the top.

5. Cover, leaving the lid ajar about 1 inch to allow steam to escape, and simmer slowly for at least 5 hours; ten hours are even better if you will be around to turn off the heat.

6. When the stock has finished cooking, allow it to come to room temperature. Refrigerate the stock, uncovered, overnight.

7. When the fat has hardened on the surface of the stock, remove it. Warm the defatted stock until it becomes liquid.

8. Strain the liquid and taste. If the flavor of the stock is too weak, boil it down to evaporate more of the liquid and concentrate its strength.

9. Store the stock in the freezer in the size container you will be using most frequently. You can then take the stock directly from the freezer and melt it whenever you need it.

Makes about 2½ quarts (10 cups) stock.

Fish Stock

2 pounds fish heads, bones and trimmings
2½ quarts distilled water
3 onions, sliced
6 parsley sprigs
1 carrot, scraped and sliced
1 teaspoon dried marjoram
¼ teaspoon peppercorns
¼ cup fresh lemon juice

1. Bring all ingredients to a boil and simmer, uncovered, for 45 minutes.

2. Line a colander or strainer with damp cheesecloth and strain the fish stock through it.

3. Cool to room temperature and store in the refrigerator. If you are not planning to use the fish stock within 2 days, store it in the freezer.

Makes 2 quarts (8 cups) stock.

White Sauce

1 cup milk
2 tablespoons butter or corn oil margarine
1½ tablespoons sifted all-purpose flour
⅛ teaspoon salt

1. Put the milk in a saucepan on low heat and bring to the boiling point.

2. In another saucepan, melt the margarine and add the flour, stirring constantly. Cook, stirring, for 3 minutes. *Do not brown.*

3. Remove the flour and margarine mixture from the heat and add the simmering milk all at once, stirring constantly with a wire whisk.

4. Put the sauce back on low heat and cook slowly until thickened, stirring occasionally.

5. Add the salt and mix thoroughly. If there are lumps in the sauce, whirl it in a blender container until smooth.

Makes 1 cup.

Hollandaise Sauce

2 egg yolks
¼ teaspoon salt
Dash cayenne pepper
½ cup melted butter or corn oil margarine
1 tablespoon freshly squeezed lemon juice

1. Beat the egg yolks, using a wire whisk or an eggbeater, until thick and very yellow. Add the salt and cayenne.

2. Start adding the melted butter or margarine slowly, about 1 teaspoon at a time, beating constantly, until you have added at least half of it.

3. Add the lemon juice to the remaining butter or margarine and mix well. Continue adding it slowly to the egg yolks, beating constantly.

Makes ½ cup.

Pizza Sauce

2 cups tomato juice
2 tablespoons red wine vinegar
¼ teaspoon salt
1 medium-size onion, thinly sliced
1 teaspoon oregano

1. Combine the tomato juice, vinegar, salt and onion in a saucepan and mix thoroughly.
2. Bring the mixture to a boil and reduce the heat. Simmer uncovered for 1 hour.
3. Add the oregano and continue to simmer uncovered for 30 minutes.

Makes 1 ample cup.

Mayonnaise

1 raw egg, at room temperature
¼ teaspoon dry mustard
½ teaspoon salt
1 tablespoon freshly squeezed lemon juice
1 cup corn oil

1. Dip the egg in boiling water for 30 seconds before breaking it.
2. Put the egg in a blender container with the dry mustard, salt, lemon juice and ¼ cup of the corn oil.
3. Turn on low speed. Immediately start pouring in the remaining oil in a steady stream.
4. Switch the blender to high speed for 3 or 4 seconds and then turn it off. Store mayonnaise in the refrigerator.

Makes 1 cup.

French Dressing

1 teaspoon salt
¼ cup red wine vinegar
¼ teaspoon pure crystalline fructose
¼ teaspoon freshly ground black pepper
1½ teaspoons freshly squeezed lemon juice
¾ teaspoon Worcestershire sauce
½ teaspoon Dijon-style mustard
½ garlic clove, minced
¼ cup water
1 cup corn oil

1. Dissolve the salt in the vinegar. Add all other ingredients except the oil and mix well.

2. Slowly stir in the oil. Pour into a jar with a tight-fitting lid and shake vigorously for 1 full minute. Store in the refrigerator.

Makes 1½ cups.

On Stocks, Sauces and Dressings

As the recipes in this chapter show, it is relatively easy to prepare your own stocks, sauces and dressings. They do make a big difference in the flavor of dishes, and they are less expensive. Canned or bottled products can also be used, of course. Prepared chicken or beef stock is often sold as chicken broth or beef broth.

On Fructose

I use fructose (a kind of sugar) in recipes because it is usually far sweeter than ordinary table sugar. It serves to heighten and sharpen flavors, especially in the absence of salt. Pure crystalline fructose is easily available in the dietetic section of your market or in health food stores.

EGG & CHEESE
STUFFED SPUDS

Many of the egg and cheese stuffed spuds are wonderful for brunch entrées. If you are entertaining, they are also practical for buffets because they are one-dish meals. One of my favorite brunch menus is Spud "Crêpes" Florentine served with sliced melon.

These recipes are also excellent budget stretchers for meatless meals for any occasion. Surprise your friends with Pizza Potatoes and a tossed green salad with Italian dressing the next time you are having guests for dinner.

Most of these recipes are good for vegetarian meal planning. A very few of them call for chicken stock as an ingredient, and it can be replaced with vegetable stock. The Runners' Stuffed Spud is a great "brown bag" lunch for vegetarian menus.

Eggs Foo Yung Spud

For an unusual approach to an oriental dinner, serve this spud as the entrée with stir-fried pea pods. Have egg-flower soup to start, and fortune cookies for dessert.

2 baked potatoes
Sauce:
   1 tablespoon soy sauce
   2 teaspoons cornstarch
   1 tablespoon rice vinegar
   ½ cup water
   1 teaspoon pure crystalline fructose
1 tablespoon corn oil
2 eggs, lightly beaten
¼ teaspoon salt
½ cup drained canned bean sprouts
¼ cup finely chopped green onion tops

1. Cut a thin slice from the top of each potato. Remove the pulp from the potatoes, being careful not to tear the shells. Place the potato pulp in a mixing bowl and mash; cover and set aside. Keep the shells warm.

2. Combine the sauce ingredients and cook over low heat, stirring constantly, until thickened (or you may warm ¼ cup of any commercial sweet-and-sour sauce). Keep sauce warm.

3. Heat the corn oil in a skillet. Add the eggs, salt, bean sprouts, green onion tops and mashed potatoes and cook until set, like scrambled eggs.

4. Heap the egg mixture into the warm potato shells and pour the sauce over the top.

Vegetarian Quiche Spud

2 baked potatoes
1 tablespoon butter or corn-oil margarine
¼ cup chopped onion
½ cup dairy sour cream
2 eggs, lightly beaten
⅛ teaspoon salt
⅛ teaspoon freshly ground black pepper
¾ cup ¼-inch cubes of Swiss cheese
1 cup chopped assorted cooked leftover vegetables
Chopped parsley for garnish

1. Cut a thin slice from the top of each potato. Remove the pulp from the potatoes, being careful not to tear the shells. Place the potato pulp in a mixing bowl and mash; cover and set aside. Set the shells aside.

2. Heat the butter or margarine in a skillet. Add the onion and cook over low heat until tender, about 10 minutes. Add the sour cream, lightly beaten eggs, salt and pepper, stirring constantly. Add the mashed potatoes and mix well. Add the cubed Swiss cheese and assorted cooked vegetables and mix lightly.

3. Heap the mixture into the potato shells. Bake at 350°F. for 45 minutes. Garnish with chopped parsley just before serving.

Variation: Substitute ½ cup cooked ham-flavored textured vegetable protein granules for ½ cup of the chopped vegetables.

Potato-Cheese
Soufflé in Spuds

2 baked potatoes
½ cup milk, at the boiling point
2 tablespoons butter or corn-oil margarine
1 tablespoon all-purpose flour
1 egg yolk
½ cup grated sharp Cheddar cheese
¼ teaspoon salt
Pinch of white pepper
¼ teaspoon Worcestershire sauce
3 egg whites, at room temperature
⅛ teaspoon cream of tartar

1. Cut a thin slice from the top of each potato. Remove the pulp from the potatoes, being careful not to tear the shells. Place the pota-to pulp in a mixing bowl and mash; cover and set aside. Spread the shells out as liners in 4-inch ovenproof bowls or soufflé dishes.

2. Preheat the oven to 400°F. Pour the milk into a small saucepan over low heat. Melt the butter or corn-oil margarine in another saucepan. Add the flour to the fat, stirring constantly for 3 minutes. *Do not brown!*

3. Take the flour/butter mixture off the heat and pour in the boil-ing milk all at once, stirring with a wire whisk. Put the pan back on the heat and allow sauce to come to a boil, stirring constantly. Boil for 1 minute. Remove from the heat and add the egg yolk, stirring in thoroughly.

4. Add the cheese and mix thoroughly. Add salt, pepper and Worcestershire sauce. Add ¾ cup of the mashed potato and mix thoroughly. (Store the remaining mashed potato for another meal.)

5. Combine the egg whites and cream of tartar and beat until stiff but not dry. Add one quarter of the egg whites to the potato-cheese mixture and stir them in. Add remaining egg whites and carefully fold them in, being sure not to overmix.

26

6. Spoon the mixture into the potato shells in the bowls or soufflé dishes and place in the 400°F. oven. Immediately turn the oven down to 375°F. and bake for 15 to 20 minutes. Serve immediately. Remember the old saying: "It is better to wait for a soufflé because a soufflé will not wait for you."

Tofu Stuffed Spud

2 baked potatoes
1 cup tofu (½ pound)
1 egg, lightly beaten
1 teaspoon seasoned salt
½ cup chopped green onions
½ cup dairy sour cream
½ cup grated Cheddar cheese

1. Cut a thin slice from the top of each potato. Remove the pulp from the potatoes, being careful not to tear the shells. Keep the shells warm. Add the tofu to the potato pulp and mash together until thoroughly mixed.

2. Combine the beaten egg and seasoned salt and add to the potato-tofu mixture; mix well. Add all other ingredients and mix well.

3. Heap into the warm potato shells and bake at 350°F. for 45 minutes.

Banana Breakfast Spud

This is also a nutritious after-school snack or an unusual light supper entrée.

2 baked potatoes
1 cup ricotta or cottage cheese
2 tablespoons pure crystalline fructose
1½ teaspoons vanilla extract
1 teaspoon freshly grated lemon rind
1 teaspoon fresh lemon juice
2 ripe bananas, mashed
Ground cinnamon for garnish (optional)
Cinnamon sticks for garnish (optional)

1. Cut the potatoes into halves and let them cool to room temperature. Remove the potato pulp, being careful not to tear the shells.

2. Place the potato pulp and all other ingredients except the garnish in a blender container and blend until smooth.

3. Spoon the mixture into the potato shells and garnish with ground cinnamon. Place a cinnamon stick in each potato half.

Runners' Stuffed Spud

The Runners' Stuffed Spud is a wonderful pick-me-up for marathon runners or just-beginning joggers to have on returning home. It is good for breakfast, lunch, dinner or just a high-energy snack.

2 tablespoons sunflower seeds
2 baked potatoes
¼ cup milk
2 tablespoons honey
½ cup low-fat cottage cheese
1 apple, finely chopped
¼ cup raisins
½ teaspoon ground cinnamon
1 teaspoon vanilla extract

1. Toast the sunflower seeds on the center rack of a 350°F. oven for 8 to 10 minutes, or until golden brown. Watch them carefully as they burn easily. Set aside.

2. Cut a thin slice from the top of each potato. Remove the pulp from the potatoes, being careful not to tear the shells. Add the milk and honey to the potato pulp and mash thoroughly.

3. Add the remaining ingredients, including toasted sunflower seeds, and mix well.

4. Heap the mixture into the potato shells. Serve immediately or refrigerate until cold.

Canyon Ranch Stuft Spud

This potato is a popular luncheon entrée at the Canyon Ranch Vacation/Fitness Resort in Tucson, Arizona.

2 baked small potatoes
1 medium-size onion, finely chopped
¼ cup Chicken Stock, defatted (see Index)
½ cup low-fat cottage cheese
2 tablespoons grated Parmesan cheese
2 tablespoons snipped chives or green onion tops

1. Cut a very thin slice from the top of each potato. Remove the pulp from the potatoes, being careful not to tear the shells. Place the pulp in a mixing bowl and mash; cover and set aside. Keep the shells warm.

2. Sauté the onion in the chicken stock until clear and tender. Add the mashed potato, cottage cheese and Parmesan cheese to the cooked onion. Mix well and heat thoroughly.

3. Heap the potato mixture into the warm shells.

4. To serve, sprinkle the top of each Stuft Spud with 1 tablespoon of snipped chives or green onion tops.

If you have prepared potatoes in advance, heat in a 350°F. oven for 10 to 15 minutes, or until hot, before adding the chives.

Potato Primavera Spud

The inspiration for Potato Primavera Spud obviously came from Pasta Primavera and you will be surprised to find you may like it even better.

2 tablespoons pine nuts
2 baked potatoes
½ cup White Sauce (see Index)
⅛ teaspoon salt
¼ cup Parmesan cheese
¼ cup cooked peas
¼ cup diced cooked carrots
¼ cup diced cooked yellow squash
½ cup cooked small broccoli flowerets
½ cup cooked chopped onion
1 small tomato, peeled and diced

1. Toast the pine nuts in a 350°F. oven for 8 to 10 minutes, or until golden brown. Watch them carefully as they burn easily. Set aside.

2. Cut a thin slice from the top of each potato. Remove the pulp from the potatoes, being careful not to tear the shells. Keep the shells warm.

3. Crumble the potato pulp. Add the white sauce, salt and Parmesan cheese and mix thoroughly. Add all other vegetables except the tomatoes and mix well. Add the pine nuts and mix thoroughly.

4. Heap into the warm potato shells. Garnish each potato with some diced tomato.

Variations: You may vary the vegetables according to what you have on hand. It is best to have a colorful combination, all cooked just crisp-tender. You may either heat the white sauce and the vegetables before adding them to the crumbled potato pulp, or add them cold and put the stuffed potato in a 350°F. oven for 10 to 15 minutes before garnishing with the tomato.

V getable Stuff d Spud

2 baked potatoes
½ cup White Sauce (see Index)
¼ teaspoon salt
½ cup grated Monterey Jack cheese
¼ cup cooked peas (if frozen, thaw them first)
¼ cup chopped cooked carrots
2 tablespoons chopped green bell pepper
1 tablespoon diced pimiento

1. Cut the baked potatoes into halves. Scoop out the pulp, mash well, and set aside in a covered bowl.

2. Combine all other ingredients and mix well. Stir into the mashed potato and again mix well.

3. Heap the mixture into the potato halves. Place them on an ungreased cookie sheet, and bake in a 375°F. oven for 20 to 25 minutes, or until the tops are brown.

Beer and Pretzel Spud

2 baked potatoes
⅓ cup beer, your favorite brand
¼ cup Cheddar-type cheese spread
¼ teaspoon salt
Pretzel sticks for garnish

1. Cut a thin slice from the top of each potato. Remove the pulp from the potatoes, being careful not to tear the shells. Place the potato pulp in a mixing bowl and mash; cover and set aside. Keep the shells warm.

2. Combine the beer and the cheese spread in a saucepan and cook over low heat until the cheese is completely melted. Add the mashed potato and salt and mix thoroughly, stirring constantly until the mixture is heated through.

3. Heap the mixture into the warm potato shells and garnish with broken pretzel sticks. This speedy spud can be made in minutes and enjoyed with the rest of the can of cold beer while watching Monday night football.

Rarebit in a Spud

2 baked potatoes
⅔ cup canned condensed Cheddar cheese soup
2 dashes of Tabasco
¼ cup sliced ripe olives
¼ cup pimiento strips
⅛ teaspoon salt
⅛ teaspoon pepper
Chopped parsley for garnish

1. Cut a thin slice from the top of each potato. Remove the pulp from the potatoes, being careful not to tear the shells. Place the potato pulp in a mixing bowl and mash; cover and set aside. Keep the shells warm.

2. Heat the soup and Tabasco in a saucepan. Add the mashed potato pulp, mixing well. Add the olives, pimiento, salt and pepper; stir lightly and heat thoroughly.

3. Heap the mixture into the warm potato shells and garnish with chopped parsley.

Potato Onion Soup au Gratin

2 baked potatoes
1 can (10½ ounces) condensed onion soup
½ cup grated Gruyère or Swiss cheese

1. Cut a thin slice from the top of each potato. Remove the pulp from the potatoes, being careful not to tear the shells. Place the potato pulp in a mixing bowl and mash. Keep the shells warm.

2. Combine the onion soup with the potato pulp and mix thoroughly.

3. Spoon the potato and soup mixture into the warm potato "bowls" and top each with ¼ cup of the grated cheese.

4. Bake in a 375°F. oven for 20 minutes, or until the cheese is lightly browned.

Spud "Crêpes" Florentine

2 baked potatoes
½ cup ricotta cheese
¼ cup milk
¼ teaspoon garlic powder
⅛ teaspoon salt
1 cup chopped cooked drained spinach
2 tablespoons Parmesan cheese

1. Cut a thin slice from the top of each potato. Remove the pulp from the potatoes, being careful not to tear the shells. Place the potato pulp in a mixing bowl. Keep the shells warm.

2. Add the cheese, milk, garlic powder and salt to the mashed potatoes and mix well. Add the spinach and again mix well.

3. Heap the mixture into the warm potato shells and top with Parmesan cheese.

4. Bake in a 350°F. oven for 20 minutes.

Variations: In a hurry, use one 10-ounce package of frozen chopped spinach, thawed. Use 1 cup chopped broccoli in place of the spinach.

Enchiladas de Papas

(Potato Enchiladas)

Enchiladas de Papas may be the next Mexican classic. If you don't have any tortillas and you feel like eating an enchilada, you will find Enchiladas de Papas *fantástico!*

2 baked potatoes
1 tablespoon corn oil
1 small onion, finely chopped
½ teaspoon salt
¼ teaspoon ground cuminseed
1 teaspoon chili powder
¼ cup Chicken Stock (see Index)
1 large tomato, peeled and diced
½ cup grated Cheddar cheese

1. Slit the tops of the baked potatoes and carefully remove the pulp. Spoon the pulp into a bowl and mash thoroughly; cover and set aside. Keep the shells warm.

2. Heat the oil in a skillet. Add the chopped onion and cook over low heat until clear and soft, about 10 minutes.

3. Add the salt, cuminseed, chili powder and chicken stock and mix well. Add the tomato and mashed potato and mix well. Cook over low heat for 5 minutes. Add ¼ cup of the cheese and mix thoroughly, heating through.

4. Heap the enchilada filling into the warm potato shells. Sprinkle the top of each potato with 2 tablespoons of grated cheese.

5. Bake in a 350°F. oven until the cheese is melted.

Papas Refritos con Queso

(Refried Potatoes with Cheese)

Once you have tried this, you may never want refried beans again!

2 baked potatoes
1 tablespoon corn oil
1 small onion
2 garlic cloves, minced
2 teaspoons chili powder
¼ teaspoon salt
½ cup tomato sauce
Dash of Tabasco (optional)
1 cup grated sharp Cheddar cheese or Monterey Jack cheese

1. Cut a thin slice from the top of each potato. Remove the pulp from the potatoes, being careful not to tear the shells. Place the potato pulp in a mixing bowl and mash; cover and set aside. Keep the shells warm.

2. Heat the oil in a skillet. Add the onion and garlic and cook over low heat until soft, about 10 minutes. Add the chili powder and salt and mix well.

3. Add the mashed potatoes to the skillet mixture and mix thoroughly. Cook, stirring frequently, for 5 minutes.

4. Add the tomato sauce, Tabasco if you use it, and ¾ cup of the cheese; mix well.

5. Heap the "refried" potatoes into the shells and top each potato with 2 tablespoons of grated cheese.

6. Bake in a 350°F. oven for 5 minutes, or until the cheese has melted.

Variation: *Bean Burrito Spud:* Add 1 cup mashed cooked pinto beans in step 3 with the mashed potatoes.

Pizza Potato

After having a Pizza Potato you may be spoiled forever for regular pizza.

2 baked potatoes
2 tablespoons corn-oil margarine or olive oil
2 teaspoons grated Parmesan cheese
1 teaspoon orégano, crushed in a mortar with a pestle
Salt
Pepper
1 cup Pizza Sauce (see Index)
¼ pound mozzarella cheese, grated (1 cup grated)

1. Cut the potatoes into halves lengthwise. Using a knife, cut slits about ½ inch apart in the edges of the potato shells and flatten the potato halves to form the bases for the other ingredients. Place shells on a cookie sheet.

2. Using a fork, work 1½ teaspoons of margarine or olive oil, ½ teaspoon Parmesan cheese, ¼ teaspoon orégano and pinches of salt and pepper into the potato pulp of each "pizza" base. Spread ¼ cup of pizza sauce on top of each base, and top with ¼ cup grated cheese.

3. Bake in a 400°F. oven for 10 to 15 minutes, or until the cheese is completely melted. If you wish your pizza lightly browned, put it under the broiler for 2 minutes before serving.

Variations: Add thin slices of pepperoni or sausage, anchovies, mushrooms, green pepper, or any other topping you particularly like on pizza, on top of the cheese. You can use canned pizza sauce if you're in a hurry.

Potato Relleno

Potato Relleno was inspired by the classic Mexican dish, Chile Relleno, and it is equally delicious.

2 baked potatoes
¼ cup Chicken Stock (see Index)
2 ounces Monterey Jack cheese, grated (1 cup grated)
1 can (4 ounces) Ortega chiles, seeds removed and chopped
¼ teaspoon salt
½ teaspoon ground cuminseed
1 egg, separated

1. Slit the tops of the potatoes and carefully remove the pulp. Keep the potato shells warm.

2. Mash the potato pulp and add the chicken stock, grated Jack cheese, chopped chiles, salt and cuminseed; mix thoroughly.

3. Stuff the mixture into the baked potato shells, and press potatoes closed.

4. Bake in a preheated 400°F. oven for 10 minutes, or until the cheese is completely melted.

5. Beat the egg white until stiff but not dry. Beat the egg yolk until smooth and fold the yolk into the egg white. Spoon half of the egg mixture over the top of each potato.

6. Place the potatoes under the broiler until lightly browned.

Variations: *Potato Chicken Relleno:* Add 1 cup chopped cooked chicken in step 2.
Vegetarian "Chicken" Relleno: Add ½ cup chopped chicken-flavored textured vegetable protein (¼ cup uncooked) in step 2.

Northern Italian Stuffed Spud

2 baked potatoes
1 tablespoon olive oil
1 small onion, finely chopped
1 small carrot, scraped and finely chopped
2 tablespoons finely chopped parsley
¼ cup dry white wine
½ teaspoon salt
⅛ teaspoon white pepper
¼ teaspoon orégano, crushed in a mortar with a pestle
¼ teaspoon basil, crushed in a mortar with a pestle
½ cup White Sauce (see Index)
2 tablespoons Parmesan cheese
⅛ teaspoon grated nutmeg
Chopped parsley for garnish (optional)

1. Cut a thin slice from the top of each potato. Remove the pulp from the potatoes, being careful not to tear the shells. Place the potato pulp in a mixing bowl and crumble; cover and set aside. Keep the shells warm.

2. Heat the oil in a skillet. Add the onion, carrot and parsley and cook over low heat until tender, about 10 minutes.

3. Combine the wine, seasoning and herbs, and add to the vegetables. Simmer until the wine is completely absorbed. Remove from the heat.

4. Combine the white sauce, Parmesan cheese and nutmeg and mix well. Add the white sauce mixture, crumbled potatoes and cooked vegetables, and mix well. Place back on the heat until heated through.

5. Heap the mixture into the warm potato shells. Garnish with chopped parsley.

Variation: *Sweetbread Stuffed Spud:* Add ½ cup chopped cooked veal sweetbread to the mixture in step 4.

41

FISH & SEAFOOD STUFFED SPUDS

Fish and seafood stuffed spuds are delightfully different. Many people who aren't crazy about fish will be pleasantly surprised at how good the combination of potatoes and all types of fish and seafood is.

The Shrimp Salad in a Spud is a superb luncheon entrée and certainly an unusual approach to potato salad.

The Dilled Fish Stuffed Spud Amandine is my favorite recipe for using leftover fish and is also a good entrée for buffets because it is so easy to serve.

Dill d Fish Stuff d Spud Amandine

¼ cup chopped raw almonds
2 baked potatoes
¼ cup Mayonnaise (see Index)
½ cup dairy sour cream
¼ teaspoon salt
¼ teaspoon tarragon, crushed in a mortar with a pestle
½ teaspoon dried dillweed, crushed in a mortar with a pestle
1 cup chopped cooked fish (any leftover fish will do)

1. Toast the almonds in a 350°F. oven for 8 to 10 minutes, or until golden brown. Watch them carefully as they burn easily. Set aside.

2. Cut a thin slice from the top of each potato. Remove the pulp from the potatoes, being careful not to tear the shells. Place the potato pulp in a bowl and mash. Keep the shells warm.

3. Add the mayonnaise, sour cream, salt, tarragon and dillweed to the mashed potatoes and mix thoroughly. Add the fish and toasted almonds, reserving enough of the almonds to sprinkle over the tops for garnish.

4. Heap the mixture into the potato shells. Heat in a 350°F. oven for 15 minutes. Garnish with the reserved almonds before serving.

Variations: *Chicken with Dill Sauce in a Spud:* Substitute 2 tablespoons sunflower seeds for the almonds (toast the same way), and 1 cup chopped cooked chicken for the fish; garnish with fresh dill if available.

Vegetarian "Chicken" with Dill Sauce in a Spud: Substitute ½ cup cooked chicken-flavored textured vegetable protein (¼ cup uncooked) for the chopped chicken in the first variation.

Fish Véronique Stuffed Spud

2 baked potatoes
½ cup White Sauce (see Index)
2 tablespoons sherry
1 cup chopped cooked firm white fish
1 can (8½ ounces) seedless grapes, drained
⅛ teaspoon salt
⅛ teaspoon white pepper
Seedless grapes for garnish

1. Cut a thin slice from the top of each potato. Remove the pulp from the potatoes, being careful not to tear the shells. Place the potato pulp in a mixing bowl. Set the shells aside.

2. Add the white sauce and sherry to the potato pulp and mash thoroughly.

3. Add the fish, grapes, salt and pepper to the potato mixture and mix well.

4. Heap the mixture into the potato shells. Heat in a 350°F. oven for 15 minutes. Garnish with seedless grapes.

Variation: *Chicken Véronique Stuffed Spud:* Substitute 1 cup chopped cooked chicken for the chopped fish.

Bouillabaisse Stuffed Spud

Marseilles, on the south coast of France, is the undisputed bouillabaisse capital of the world; however, there is a great difference of
opinion as to what ingredients are essential to make it "authentic."
Around Marseilles you won't find shellfish in bouillabaisse, so this
Bouillabaisse Stuffed Spud is at least half authentic. They serve theirs
with crusty bread and this one is served in a spud.

¼ pound fresh white fish
2 teaspoons fresh lemon juice
Salt
2 baked potatoes
1 tablespoon corn oil
1 small onion, thinly sliced
¼ cup chopped leek, white part only
1 garlic clove, finely chopped
1 tomato, peeled, seeded and diced
1 tablespoon chopped parsley
¼ cup chopped celery
1 bay leaf
½ teaspoon salt
⅛ teaspoon ground fennel seed
⅛ teaspoon dried thyme
⅛ teaspoon ground saffron
Pinch of freshly ground black pepper
½ cup Chicken Stock or Fish Stock (see Index)
1 cup dry white wine
Parsley sprigs for garnish (optional)

1. Wash the fish in cold water and pat dry. Cut into bite-size pieces. Sprinkle with lemon juice and salt lightly. Set aside.

2. Cut a thin slice from the top of each potato. Remove the pulp
from the potatoes, being careful not to tear the shells. Crumble the
potato pulp and cover. Keep the shells warm.

3. Heat the corn oil in a skillet. Add all vegetables, herbs and seasonings; mix thoroughly. Cook over low heat for 3 minutes. Add the

stock and wine and bring to a boil. Simmer for 10 more minutes, reducing the liquid by half.

4. Add the fish and continue to boil until the fish has turned white, about 5 minutes.

5. Remove the bay leaf and add the crumbled potato pulp. Mix thoroughly and heap into the warm potato shells.

Classic Caviar Spud

This is a glamorous entrée to serve on your yacht, at your beach house or at your weekend hideaway in the mountains. It is simple to prepare and all of the ingredients can be easily packed to take with you. Also, it takes very little kitchen space for preparation. It can also be an elegant entrée for a candlelight dinner for two, served with a cold watercress salad, fruit marinated in Grand Marnier for dessert and of course a bottle of chilled Champagne.

2 baked potatoes
1 cup dairy sour cream
1 hard-cooked egg, finely chopped
¼ cup finely chopped onion
2 ounces red caviar
Watercress for garnish (optional)

1. Cut a thin slice from the top of each potato. Remove the pulp from the potatoes, being careful not to tear the shells.

2. Combine potato pulp and sour cream and mash well. Add chopped egg and onion and mix thoroughly.

3. Heap the potato mixture in the potato shells and top each potato with 2 tablespoons of caviar. The Classic Caviar Spud is good served hot or cold.

4. Garnish with watercress if desired.

47

Crab and Swiss Cheese Spud

¼ cup slivered almonds
2 baked potatoes
1 tablespoon corn oil
¼ cup sliced green onions
1 teaspoon dry mustard
1 teaspoon grated lemon rind
½ cup grated Swiss cheese
Pinch of ground mace
½ teaspoon salt
⅛ teaspoon freshly ground black pepper
½ cup milk
¾ cup chopped fresh crab meat
Chopped parsley for garnish
Chopped pimiento for garnish (optional)

1. Toast the almonds in a 350°F. oven for 8 to 10 minutes, or until golden brown. Watch them carefully as they burn easily. Set aside.

2. Cut a thin slice from the top of each potato. Remove the pulp from the potatoes, being careful not to tear the shells. Place the potato pulp in a mixing bowl and mash; cover and set aside. Keep the shells warm.

3. Heat the corn oil in a skillet. Add the onions and cook until tender, about 10 minutes.

4. Combine the mustard, lemon rind, grated cheese, mace and salt and pepper and set aside. Heat the milk; add it to the mashed potatoes and mix thoroughly.

5. Add the potato mixture and the cheese mixture to the onions in the skillet, stirring lightly until the cheese is melted and the mixture is thoroughly heated.

6. Add the crab meat and almonds and stir until the crab meat is heated.

7. Heap the mixture into the warm potato shells. Garnish with parsley or pimiento or both.

Variation: Instead of fresh crab, use 6 ounces canned crab meat, flaked. In step 6, do not stir vigorously or crab will become mushy.

Curried Crab in Spuds

2 baked potatoes
1 tablespoon butter or corn-oil margarine
½ cup chopped onion
¼ cup Mayonnaise (see Index)
¼ cup dairy sour cream
1½ teaspoons curry powder
½ teaspoon salt
⅛ teaspoon ground ginger
½ cup crushed pineapple, drained
¾ cup diced fresh crab meat

1. Cut a thin slice from the top of each potato. Remove the pulp from the potatoes, being careful not to tear the shells. Place the potato pulp in a mixing bowl and crumble; cover and set aside. Keep the shells warm.

2. Heat the butter or margarine in a large skillet. Add the onion and cook over low heat until tender, about 10 minutes.

3. Combine the mayonnaise, sour cream, curry powder, salt and ginger and mix well. Stir the mayonnaise mixture into the potatoes.

4. Combine all ingredients in the skillet, mix well, and heat through.

5. Heap the mixture into the warm potato shells and serve immediately.

49

Spud Oscar

2 baked potatoes
2 tablespoons butter or corn-oil margarine
½ teaspoon salt
⅛ teaspoon freshly ground black pepper
12 asparagus spears, steamed crisp-tender
2 cooked large crab legs
¾ cup Hollandaise Sauce (see Index)

1. Cut the potatoes into halves. With a knife, slit the edges of the potato shells at 1-inch intervals, and flatten the shells and pulp to form the 4 bases for the other ingredients.

2. Work 1½ teaspoons of butter or margarine, ⅛ teaspoon of salt and a pinch of pepper into each potato half with a fork.

3. Place 3 asparagus spears on each potato half. Place ½ crab leg on each potato half. Top each with 3 tablespoons of hollandaise sauce. Serve cold or at room temperature.

Shrimp Salad in a Spud

2 baked potatoes
2 teaspoons lemon juice
2 tablespoons olive oil
⅛ teaspoon salt
⅛ teaspoon freshly ground black pepper
1 cup cooked shelled shrimps, coarsely chopped, or 1 cup small
    frozen shrimps, drained and dried
½ cup torn lettuce, in small pieces
2 tablespoons minced green onion
½ medium-size tomato, peeled and diced
½ small avocado, peeled and cubed
2 teaspoons finely chopped parsley

1. Cut a thin slice from the top of each potato. Allow potatoes to cool to room temperature. Remove the pulp from the potatoes, being careful not to tear the shells. Dice the potato pulp and place in a mixing bowl.

2. Combine the lemon juice, oil, salt and pepper and mix well. Set aside.

3. Add the shrimps, lettuce, green onion, tomato, avocado and parsley to the diced potato and mix thoroughly. Pour the lemon juice mixture over the potato mixture and toss lightly.

4. Heap the mixture into the potato shells. This is best when served immediately; however, if you wish to make them ahead of time, they can be refrigerated and served cold.

Oyster Stew Spuds

2 baked potatoes
2 tablespoons butter or corn-oil margarine
¼ cup finely chopped onion
¼ cup finely chopped celery
1 garlic clove, finely chopped
½ cup cream or milk
½ teaspoon salt
⅛ teaspoon white pepper
1 cup chopped oysters
Parsley sprigs for garnish

1. Cut a thin slice from the top of each potato. Remove the pulp from the potatoes, being careful not to tear the shells. Place in a mixing bowl; cover and set aside. Keep the shells warm.

2. Melt the corn-oil margarine in a saucepan. Add the onion, celery and garlic and cook until soft.

3. While the vegetables are cooking, whip the potato pulp with a mixer and add the milk, salt and pepper; mix well. Set aside.

4. Add the chopped oysters to the sautéed vegetables and cook until the oysters turn white. Add the whipped potato to the oyster mixture and mix thoroughly.

5. Spoon the mixture into the warm potato shells and garnish with parsley sprigs. Serve immediately.

Spicy Clam Stuffed Spud

2 baked potatoes
1 tablespoon corn oil
½ cup chopped onion
2 garlic cloves, minced
½ cup tomato sauce
¼ cup dry red wine
¼ cup sliced ripe olives
1 teaspoon lemon juice
½ teaspoon salt
¼ teaspoon pepper
2 dashes of Tabasco (optional)
1 can (6½ ounces) chopped clams, drained
Parsley sprigs for garnish (optional)

1. Cut a thin slice from the top of each potato. Remove the pulp from the potatoes, being careful not to tear the shells. Place the potato pulp in a mixing bowl and mash; cover and set aside. Keep the shells warm.

2. Heat the corn oil in a large skillet. Add the onion and garlic and cook over low heat until tender, about 10 minutes.

3. Combine the tomato sauce, red wine, olives, lemon juice, salt and pepper, and Tabasco if you use it, and add to the onion mixture in the skillet. Cook for an additional 5 minutes.

4. Add the mashed potatoes and mix thoroughly. Add chopped clams and cook until the mixture is heated to serving temperature.

5. Heap the mixture into the warm potato shells and serve immediately. Garnish with parsley sprigs if desired.

Speedy Clam Spud

2 baked potatoes
½ package (⅓ cup) dehydrated leek soup mix (Knorr or other
    brand)
½ cup boiling water
1 can (6½ ounces) chopped clams, drained
⅛ teaspoon pepper
Chopped parsley for garnish

1. Cut a thin slice from the top of each potato. Remove the pulp from the potatoes, being careful not to tear the shells. Place the potato pulp in a mixing bowl and mash; cover and set aside. Keep the shells warm.

2. Combine the leek soup mix and water and mix well. Add the mashed potato, chopped clams and pepper, and heat through.

3. Heap the mixture into the warm potato shells. Garnish with chopped parsley.

Seafood Curry with Capers Spud

2 baked potatoes
1 tablespoon corn oil
¼ cup chopped onion
1½ teaspoons curry powder
2 cans (4½ ounces each) seafood (crab, lobster, shrimp)
½ cup milk
¼ cup capers, drained
Cayenne pepper for garnish (optional)

1. Cut a thin slice from the top of each potato. Remove the pulp from the potatoes, being careful not to tear the shells. Place the potato pulp in a mixing bowl and mash; cover and set aside. Keep the shells warm.

2. Heat the corn oil in a large skillet. Cook the onion over low heat until tender, about 10 minutes.

3. Add the curry powder and seafood to the onion in the skillet. Stir lightly.

4. Add the milk to the mashed potato and mix well. Add to the ingredients in the skillet, lightly folding and heating through. Add the capers and mix well.

5. Heap the mixture into the warm potato shells and garnish very lightly with cayenne pepper.

Seafood Stew Spud

2 baked potatoes
2 tablespoons butter or corn-oil margarine
¼ cup finely chopped onion
¼ cup finely chopped celery
1 garlic clove, finely chopped
½ cup cream or milk
½ teaspoon salt
⅛ teaspoon white pepper
1 cup chopped shrimps, crab, lobster or leftover fish, or a
    combination
Parsley sprigs for garnish

1. Cut a thin slice from the top of each potato. Remove the pulp from the potatoes, being careful not to tear the shells. Place in a mixing bowl, cover and set aside. Keep the shells warm.

2. Melt the butter or margarine in a saucepan. Add the onion, celery and garlic and cook until soft, about 10 minutes.

3. While the vegetables are cooking, whip the potato pulp with a mixer and add the cream or milk, salt and pepper; mix well. Set aside.

4. Add the chopped seafood to the sautéed vegetables and cook until the fish is thoroughly heated. Add the whipped potato to the fish mixture, mix thoroughly, and heat through.

5. Heap the mixture into the warm potato shells and garnish with parsley sprigs.

Gravlax Stuffed Spud

2 baked potatoes
¼ cup cider vinegar
2 teaspoons dry mustard
1 egg, lightly beaten
¼ cup milk
1 tablespoon butter or corn-oil margarine
1 tablespoon pure crystalline fructose
1 cup chopped Gravlax (Scandinavian Pickled Salmon) (recipe
  follows)
Fresh dill or parsley sprigs for garnish (optional)

1. Cut a thin slice from the top of each potato. Remove the pulp from the potatoes, being careful not to tear the shells. Crumble the potatoes and set aside in a covered bowl. Set the shells aside.

2. Combine the vinegar and mustard and stir until mustard is completely dissolved. Add the beaten egg and milk and mix well.

3. Pour the mixture into a saucepan and slowly bring to a boil, stirring constantly with a wire whisk. Continue stirring and allow to simmer for no more than 1 minute. Remove from the heat and put the butter on top of the sauce. *Do not stir!* Allow to cool to room temperature. Add the fructose and again stir with a wire whisk until thoroughly mixed.

4. Combine the potato, mustard sauce and gravlax and heap into the potato shells. Garnish with fresh dill if available, or parsley sprigs. Serve at room temperature.

Variation: Cut the potatoes into halves and then each half into halves again for 8 servings as first course or to serve with cocktails. Your Scandinavian friends will be delighted!

Gravlax

(Scandinavian Pickled Salmon)

If you are unable to find gravlax in a delicatessen, here is a recipe.

1 teaspoon dried dillweed
1 teaspoon dill seed
2 tablespoons salt
2 teaspoons pure crystalline fructose
¼ teaspoon freshly ground black pepper
2 pounds fresh salmon (a center section fillet with the skin is best)
¾ cup red wine vinegar

1. Using a mortar and pestle, crush the dillweed and dill seed, salt, fructose and black pepper together thoroughly. Sprinkle half of this mixture in the bottom of a glass dish just large enough to hold the salmon.

2. Place the salmon, skin side down, in the dish and rub the remaining herb mixture into the fish well, using your hands.

3. Pour the vinegar over the fish and cover tightly with plastic wrap or aluminum foil. Place a weight of at least 1 pound on top of the fish (I use a can of fruit or vegetables for this purpose).

4. Refrigerate for at least 2 days, spooning the juices over the marinating salmon as frequently as possible (at least five times a day).

Lox 'n' Spuds

Lox 'n' Spuds will replace Lox 'n' Bagels for real potato fanciers. Try it, you'll love it!

2 baked potatoes
2 tablespoons butter or corn-oil margarine
½ cup dairy sour cream
½ teaspoon salt
Freshly ground black pepper
4 slices of red onion
3 ounces smoked salmon (lox)
4 tablespoons cream cheese, softened
Sour cream for garnish

1. Cut the potatoes into halves. With a knife slit the edges of the potato shells at 1-inch intervals, and flatten the shells and pulp to form the 4 bases (the "bagels") for the other ingredients. Using a fork, work 1½ teaspoons of butter or margarine, 2 tablespoons of sour cream, ⅛ teaspoon of salt and a dash of pepper into each potato half.

2. Place a slice of red onion on each potato half. Divide the smoked salmon evenly over the 4 portions, reserving a small amount for topping.

3. Spread 1 tablespoon cream cheese over the top of the salmon on each potato and top each with remaining pieces of salmon and a teaspoon of sour cream.

Sockeye Salmon Spud

2 baked potatoes
1 tablespoon butter or corn-oil margarine
1 medium-size onion, finely chopped
¼ cup Chicken Stock (see Index)
Pinch of white pepper
¼ teaspoon salt
1 teaspoon Worcestershire sauce
1 tablespoon freshly squeezed lemon juice
1 can (7¾ ounces) sockeye salmon, drained and flaked
½ cup dairy sour cream
Chopped parsley for garnish (optional)

1. Cut a thin slice from the top of each potato. Remove the pulp from the potatoes, being careful not to tear the shells. Place the potato pulp in a mixing bowl and mash; cover and set aside. Keep the shells warm.

2. Heat the butter or margarine in a skillet. Add the onion and cook over low heat until tender. Add the chicken stock, pepper, salt, Worcestershire sauce and lemon juice. Add the salmon and mix thoroughly.

3. Combine the potatoes and sour cream and mix well. Add to the salmon mixture. Heat thoroughly.

4. Heap into the warm potato shells and garnish with chopped parsley.

Baked Tuna in Spud

2 baked potatoes
1 onion, chopped
2 tablespoons butter or corn-oil margarine
½ teaspoon salt
⅛ teaspoon freshly ground black pepper
1 teaspoon basil, crushed in a mortar with a pestle
1 can (7 ounces) tuna, drained and flaked
1 large tomato, diced
½ cup milk
2 tablespoons grated Parmesan cheese

1. Cut a thin slice from the top of each potato. Remove the pulp from the potatoes, being careful not to tear the shells. Place the potato pulp in a mixing bowl and mash; cover and set aside. Keep the shells warm.

2. Sauté the onion in the butter or margarine. Add the salt, pepper, basil and tuna, and cook for 5 minutes.

3. Add the mashed potato, diced tomato and milk, and mix well.

4. Heap the mixture into the potato shells and cover each potato with 1 tablespoon Parmesan cheese.

5. Bake at 350°F. for 15 minutes.

Chopstick Tuna Spud

2 baked potatoes
½ cup canned condensed mushroom soup
1 tablespoon corn oil
¼ cup diagonal slices of celery or green pepper
¼ cup chopped onion
1 can (7 ounces) water-packed tuna, drained and flaked
1 tablespoon soy sauce
¼ cup cashews
¼ cup chow mein noodles, broken in pieces

1. Cut a thin slice from the top of each potato. Remove the pulp from the potatoes, being careful not to tear the shells. Place the potato pulp in a mixing bowl. Add the soup and mix thoroughly; set aside. Keep the shells warm.

2. Heat the corn oil in a skillet. Add the celery or green pepper and the onion and cook over low heat until tender.

3. Add the tuna, soup and potato mixture and soy sauce, and mix thoroughly. Heat through.

4. Add the cashews and toss lightly. Heap the mixture into the warm potato shells. Top with chow mein noodles.

If you are making these ahead of time, add the chow mein noodles after you have reheated the spuds in a 350°F. oven for 15 minutes.

Creamed Tuna Stuffed Spud

½ cup chopped raw almonds
2 baked potatoes
2 tablespoons butter or corn-oil margarine
¼ cup chopped onion
¼ cup chopped green pepper
1 can (7 ounces) water-packed tuna, drained
3 tablespoons dry white wine
2 tablespoons chopped pimiento
2 tablespoons chopped parsley
½ teaspoon salt
½ teaspoon freshly ground black pepper
1 cup White Sauce (see Index)
¼ cup milk
Pinch of paprika
Pimiento strips for garnish (optional)

1. Toast the chopped almonds in a 350°F. oven for 8 to 10 minutes, or until golden brown. Watch them carefully as they burn easily. Set aside.

2. Cut a thin slice from the top of each potato. Remove the pulp from the potatoes, being careful not to tear the shells. Place the potato pulp in a mixing bowl and mash; cover and set aside. Keep the shells warm.

3. Heat the butter or margarine in a large skillet. Add the onion and green pepper and cook over low heat until tender, about 10 minutes. Add the tuna, wine, pimiento, parsley, salt and pepper and mix well. Stir in the white sauce.

4. Add the milk to the mashed potato; mix well. Add to the other ingredients in the skillet and cook to serving temperature. Add the toasted almonds within the last minute of cooking.

5. Heap the mixture into the warm potato shells and garnish with paprika and pimiento strips.

Tuna Casserole Spud

2 baked potatoes
2 tablespoons butter or corn-oil margarine
¼ cup chopped onion
¼ cup chopped green pepper
¼ cup chopped celery
½ cup canned condensed cream of celery soup
¼ cup milk
2 tablespoons Mayonnaise (see Index)
1 tablespoon chopped canned pimiento
1 can (7 ounces) water-packed tuna, drained and flaked
½ teaspoon salt
⅛ teaspoon freshly ground black pepper
¼ cup grated Cheddar cheese
Snipped chives or green onion tops for garnish

1. Cut a thin slice from the top of each potato. Remove the pulp from the potatoes, being careful not to tear the shells. Place the potato pulp in a mixing bowl and mash; cover and set aside. Keep the shells warm.

2. Heat the butter or margarine in a large skillet. Add the onion, green pepper and celery and cook over low heat until tender, about 10 minutes.

3. Combine the celery soup, milk and mashed potato and mix well. Add to the skillet ingredients; stir well. Combine the mayonnaise, pimiento, tuna, salt and pepper and add to the potato mixture; heat through. Add the cheese and stir until the cheese has melted and blended with the other ingredients.

4. Heap the mixture into the warm potato shells. Garnish with snipped chives or green onion tops.

Variation: *Chicken Casserole Spud:* Substitute 1 cup chopped cooked chicken for the tuna.

Salade Niçoise Spud

2 baked potatoes
1 tomato, diced
½ cucumber, chopped
1 can (2 ounces) flat fillets of anchovy, drained and coarsely
    chopped
¼ cup coarsely chopped pitted ripe olives
2 leaves of Bibb lettuce, torn into small pieces
1 leaf of romaine lettuce, torn into small pieces
½ cup French Dressing (see Index)
2 leaves of romaine lettuce for lining potato shells
Chopped parsley for garnish

1. Cut a thin slice from the top of each potato. Cool to room temperature and remove the pulp carefully. Dice the potato pulp and place in a mixing bowl. Set the shells aside.

2. Add the tomato, cucumber, anchovies, olives and torn lettuce to the diced potatoes and mix well. Add the French dressing and toss thoroughly.

3. Line the potato shells with romaine lettuce leaves and heap the salad mixture into the shells. Garnish with chopped parsley.

Salade Niçoise is best served at room temperature; however, if you are making it ahead of time, it can be refrigerated and served cold.

Jansson's Temptation in a Spud

This is an adaptation of a popular Scandinavian potato casserole. It is even more delicious when made from baked potatoes and stuffed in the spuds!

2 baked potatoes
2 tablespoons butter or corn-oil margarine
1 large onion, finely chopped
1 can (2 ounces) flat anchovy fillets, drained and finely chopped
½ cup cream or milk
⅛ teaspoon white pepper
1 tablespoon fine bread crumbs

1. Cut a thin slice from the top of each potato. Remove the pulp from the potatoes, being careful not to tear the shells. Place the potato pulp in a bowl and crumble; cover and set aside. Keep the shells warm.

2. Melt the butter or margarine in a skillet. Add the onion and cook over low heat for about 5 minutes. Add the chopped anchovies and mix thoroughly. Continue to cook for 5 more minutes, stirring frequently so that the onion does not brown.

3. Add the cream and white pepper. Mix well. Add the crumbled potatoes and again mix well. Continue cooking until most of the liquid is absorbed.

4. Heap the mixture into the warm potato shells and sprinkle 1½ teaspoons of bread crumbs over the top of each potato.

5. Bake in a 350°F. oven for 40 minutes.

This recipe is not only delicious, but so different that I selected it for the heroine of my novel, *Ambition's Woman*, an overnight Broadway star, to prepare for her favorite boyfriend, an up-and-coming young director, the first time she invited him for dinner.

POULTRY STUFFED SPUDS

Potatoes may replace dumplings in importance as a delicious combination with chicken and turkey. Poultry stuffed spuds will certainly solve all of your problems with holiday turkey leftovers. In fact the Turkey and Cranberry Spud even gives you a perfect use for leftover cranberry sauce and is a delicious entrée served hot or cold.

If you like chicken livers, you will love Chopped Chicken Livers in a Spud. I serve the pâté variation of this recipe as an hors d'oeuvre and always get compliments.

Curried Chicken in Spuds

2 baked potatoes
1 tablespoon butter or corn-oil margarine
½ cup chopped onion
½ cup Chicken Stock (see Index)
2 teaspoons curry powder
½ teaspoon salt
⅛ teaspoon ground ginger
½ cup finely chopped apple
1 cup diced cooked chicken
¼ cup milk

1. Cut a thin slice from the top of each potato. Remove the pulp from the potatoes, being careful not to tear the shells. Place the potato pulp in a mixing bowl and mash; cover and set aside. Keep the shells warm.

2. Heat the butter or margarine in a large skillet. Add the onion and cook over low heat until tender, about 10 minutes. Add the chicken stock, curry powder, salt, ginger, apple and chicken, and cook for another 10 minutes.

3. Add the milk to the potato pulp and mix thoroughly. Add the potato mixture to the ingredients in the skillet and heat thoroughly.

4. Heap the mixture into the warm potato shells and serve immediately.

Chutney and Chicken Spud

2 baked potatoes
1 tablespoon corn oil
½ cup chopped green onions, including the tops
½ cup plain yogurt
1 teaspoon curry powder
¼ cup chopped chutney
1 cup cubed cooked chicken
¼ cup chopped peanuts
Chopped egg, raisins, coconut, pineapple or any other classic
    condiments (optional)

1. Cut the potatoes into halves. Scoop out the potato pulp, being careful not to tear the shells. Mash well and set aside in a covered bowl. Keep the potato shells warm.

2. Heat the corn oil in a skillet. Add the chopped green onions and cook over low heat until tender, about 10 minutes.

3. Combine the yogurt, curry powder, chutney, mashed potato, chicken and peanuts, and add to the cooked onions in the skillet. Mix well and heat to serving temperature.

4. Heap the mixture into the warm potato shells. Serve with an assortment of classic condiments if desired.

Creamed Chicken Stuffed Spud

½ cup chopped raw almonds
2 baked potatoes
2 tablespoons butter or corn-oil margarine
¼ cup chopped onion
¼ cup chopped green pepper
1 cup chopped cooked chicken
3 tablespoons dry white wine
2 tablespoons chopped pimiento
2 tablespoons chopped parsley
½ teaspoon salt
¼ teaspoon freshly ground black pepper
1 cup White Sauce (see Index)
¼ cup milk
Pinch of paprika
Pimiento strips for garnish (optional)

1. Toast the chopped almonds in a 350°F. oven for 8 to 10 minutes, or until golden brown. Watch them carefully as they burn easily. Set aside.

2. Cut a thin slice from the top of each potato. Remove the pulp from the potatoes, being careful not to tear the shells. Place the potato pulp in a mixing bowl and mash; cover and set aside. Keep the shells warm.

3. Heat the butter or margarine in a large skillet. Add the onion and green pepper and cook over low heat until tender, about 10 minutes. Add the chicken, wine, pimiento, parsley, salt and pepper and mix well. Add the white sauce and mix well.

4. Add the milk to the mashed potato. Mix well and add to the other ingredients in the skillet. Cook to serving temperature. Add the toasted almonds within the last minute of cooking.

5. Heap mixture into warm potato shells and garnish with paprika and pimiento strips.

Chicken Tarragon Stuffed Spud

¼ cup chopped walnuts
2 baked potatoes
¼ cup Mayonnaise (see Index)
½ cup dairy sour cream
½ teaspoon salt
1 teaspoon tarragon, crushed in a mortar with a pestle
1 cup chopped cooked chicken

1. Toast the walnuts in a 350°F. oven for 8 to 10 minutes, or until golden brown. Watch them carefully as they burn easily. Set aside.

2. Cut a thin slice from the top of each potato. Remove the pulp from the potatoes, being careful not to tear the shells. Place the potato pulp in a bowl and mash. Keep the shells warm.

3. Add the mayonnaise, sour cream, salt and tarragon to the mashed potatoes and mix thoroughly. Add the chicken and toasted walnuts, reserving enough of the walnuts to sprinkle over the tops for garnish.

4. Heap the mixture into the potato shells. Bake in a 350°F. oven for 15 minutes. Garnish with the reserved walnuts before serving.

Chicken Surprise Stuffed Spud

2 baked potatoes
1 tablespoon butter or corn-oil margarine
1 cup frozen French-cut green beans, defrosted
⅓ cup milk
2 tablespoons soy sauce
½ cup dairy sour cream
1 cup cubed cooked chicken
½ cup water chestnuts, drained and thinly sliced
⅛ teaspoon paprika

1. Cut a thin slice from the top of each potato. Remove the pulp from the potatoes, being careful not to tear the shells. Place the potato pulp in a mixing bowl and mash; cover and set aside. Keep the shells warm.

2. Melt the butter or margarine in a large saucepan. Add the green beans, milk and soy sauce and heat slowly, stirring constantly. Stir in the sour cream and mashed potatoes. Add the cubed chicken and water chestnuts. Stir lightly until the mixture is heated thoroughly.

3. Heap the mixture into the warm potato shells and garnish with paprika.

Variation: *Ham Surprise Stuffed Spud:* Substitute 1 cup cubed cooked ham for the chicken.

Chicken and Cheese Spud

2 baked potatoes
1 tablespoon corn oil
¼ cup sliced green onions
1 teaspoon dry mustard
1 teaspoon grated lemon rind
½ cup grated Monterey Jack cheese
Pinch of grated nutmeg
½ teaspoon salt
⅛ teaspoon freshly ground black pepper
½ cup milk
¾ cup chopped cooked chicken
¼ cup chopped peanuts
Chopped parsley for garnish

1. Cut a thin slice from the top of each potato. Remove the pulp from the potatoes, being careful not to tear the shells. Place the potato pulp in a mixing bowl and mash; cover and set aside. Keep the shells warm.

2. Heat the corn oil in a skillet. Add the green onions and cook until tender, about 10 minutes.

3. Combine the mustard, lemon rind, grated cheese, nutmeg, salt and pepper and set aside. Heat the milk and add it to the mashed potatoes; mix thoroughly.

4. Add potato mixture and cheese mixture to the onions in the skillet, stirring lightly until the cheese is melted and the mixture is thoroughly heated.

5. Add the chicken and peanuts and stir until chicken is heated through.

6. Heap the mixture into the warm potato shells and garnish with parsley.

Chicken Florentine Stuffed Spud

2 baked potatoes
¾ cup chopped cooked spinach, drained
¾ cup chopped cooked chicken
½ cup White Sauce (see Index)
½ cup grated mozzarella cheese
⅛ teaspoon grated nutmeg
⅛ teaspoon white pepper
1 tablespoon grated Parmesan cheese

1. Cut a thin slice from the top of each potato. Remove the pulp from the potatoes, being careful not to tear the shells. Place the pota-to pulp in a bowl and mash. Keep the shells warm.

2. Add the spinach, chicken, white sauce, mozzarella cheese, nut-meg and white pepper to the mashed potatoes and mix thoroughly.

3. Heap mixture into the potato shells. Sprinkle the Parmesan cheese evenly over the tops. Bake in a 350°F. oven for 15 minutes.

Variation: *Fish Florentine Stuffed Spud:* Substitute ¾ cup cooked firm white fish, chopped, for the cooked chicken.

Chopped Chicken Livers in a Spud

2 baked potatoes
2 tablespoons butter or corn-oil margarine
½ pound fresh chicken livers
2 tablespoons brandy
½ cup Chicken Stock (see Index)
¼ teaspoon salt
¼ teaspoon freshly ground black pepper
Chopped parsley for garnish

1. Cut a thin slice from the top of each potato. Remove the pulp from the potatoes, being careful not to tear the shells. Place the potato pulp in a mixing bowl and mash; cover and set aside. Keep the shells warm.

2. Heat the butter or margarine in a skillet. Add the chicken livers and cook until tender. Chop the chicken livers coarsely and add the brandy, chicken stock, salt and pepper; mix thoroughly.

3. Add the liver mixture to the mashed potatoes and mix well. Heat the mixture thoroughly.

4. Heap into the warm potato shells and garnish with chopped parsley.

Variation: *Pâté in a Spud:* Instead of chopping the chicken livers, place the chicken livers, brandy, chicken broth, salt and pepper in a blender container and blend until smooth before adding to the mashed potatoes.

Stuffed Spud Marco Polo

2 baked potatoes
¾ cup White Sauce (see Index)
⅓ cup diced cooked turkey
⅓ cup diced cooked ham
⅓ cup chopped cooked broccoli

1. Cut a thin slice from the top of each potato. Remove the pulp from the potatoes, being careful not to tear the shells. Keep the shells warm.

2. Mash the potato pulp with ½ cup of the white sauce, reserving the remaining ¼ cup to put on the top. Add the cooked turkey, ham and broccoli, and mix gently. Heap into the warm potato shells.

3. Spoon 2 tablespoons of white sauce over each potato and put under the broiler until lightly browned.

Turkey and Cranberry Spud

Serving a Turkey and Cranberry Spud after Christmas is a marvelous way to use leftover turkey and cranberry sauce from your Christmas dinner. It is also a delicious lunch or light dinner entrée any time of the year.

2 baked potatoes
½ cup White Sauce (see Index)
½ cup canned whole-berry cranberry sauce
¾ cup chopped cooked turkey
Cranberries (from the can) for garnish

1. Cut a thin slice from the top of each potato. Remove the pulp from the potatoes, being careful not to tear the shells. Place the potato pulp in a mixing bowl and mash. Keep the shells warm.

2. Add the white sauce, cranberry sauce and chopped turkey to the potato; mix well.

3. Heap mixture into the warm potato shells and heat in 350°F. oven for 15 minutes.

4. Garnish with whole cranberries from the can before serving.

Turkey Vegetable Spud

2 baked potatoes
1 tablespoon corn oil
¼ cup sliced green onions
¼ cup shredded carrot
¼ cup chopped mushrooms
½ cup cubed cooked turkey
½ cup dairy sour cream
¼ cup milk
1 cup grated Cheddar cheese
½ cup steamed broccoli, cut into small pieces
¼ teaspoon salt
⅛ teaspoon pepper

1. Cut a thin slice from the top of each potato. Remove the pulp from the potatoes, being careful not to tear the shells. Place the potato pulp in a mixing bowl and mash; cover and set aside. Keep the shells warm.

2. Heat the corn oil in a large skillet. Add the green onion slices and cook over low heat until tender, about 10 minutes. Add the carrot, mushrooms and turkey and cook for another 10 minutes.

3. Add the sour cream and milk to the mashed potato and mix thoroughly. Add to the other ingredients in the skillet and mix well until heated through. Add ½ cup of the grated cheese and mix thoroughly as it melts.

4. Add the broccoli, salt and pepper, and mix well and heat through.

5. Heap the mixture into the warm potato shells and sprinkle the remaining cheese over the tops. Place under the broiler until the cheese is browned.

Chopped Chicken or Turkey Hash in a Spud

2 baked potatoes
1 tablespoon corn oil
¼ cup chopped onion
2 tablespoons chopped parsley
1 cup chopped cooked chicken or turkey
1 tablespoon soy sauce
⅓ cup milk
¼ teaspoon thyme, crushed in a mortar with a pestle
Chopped parsley for garnish

1. Cut a thin slice from the top of each potato. Remove the pulp from the potatoes, being careful not to tear the shells. Place the potato pulp in a saucepan and mash; cover and set aside. Keep the shells warm.

2. Heat the corn oil in a skillet. Add the onion and parsley and cook over low heat until tender, about 10 minutes.

3. Add the chopped cooked chicken or turkey and the soy sauce, and cook until the chicken or turkey is thoroughly heated. While the chicken or turkey is heating, add the milk to the mashed potato and mix well. Add the thyme and mix well. Add the potato mixture to the poultry mixture and continue to cook until the mixture is heated through, stirring well.

4. Heap the mixture into the warm potato shells and garnish with chopped parsley.

White Chili Bowl Spud

2 baked potatoes
1 tablespoon corn oil
1 medium-size onion, chopped
1 garlic clove, chopped
2 canned green Ortega chiles, seeded and chopped
½ teaspoon cuminseed
½ teaspoon orégano, crushed in a mortar with a pestle
¼ teaspoon ground coriander
¼ teaspoon salt
Pinch of cayenne pepper
½ cup cooked chopped chicken or turkey
½ cup cooked white beans
Chopped fresh cilantro or green onion tops for garnish

1. Cut a thin slice from the top of each potato. Remove the pulp from the potatoes, being careful not to tear the shells. Place the potato pulp in a bowl and crumble; cover and set aside. Keep the shells warm.

2. Heat the oil in a skillet. Cook the onion and garlic over low heat until onion is clear and tender. Add the chopped chiles and all seasonings and mix well. Add the crumbled potatoes; mix well. Cook for another 5 minutes.

3. Add the chopped chicken or turkey and the beans and heat thoroughly.

4. Heap into the warm potato shells and garnish with fresh cilantro or green onion tops.

Eclectic Salad in Potato Pockets

If you like pita pockets, you will most certainly like potato pockets. Try this recipe and then use your own imagination to make potato pockets of your own with whatever leftover bits and pieces you may have in the refrigerator.

2 baked potatoes
3 tablespoons sunflower seeds
½ cup cubed cooked chicken or turkey
¼ cup alfalfa sprouts or bean sprouts
½ cup cottage cheese
¼ cup chopped red bell pepper
¼ cup chopped green bell pepper
¼ cup chopped radishes
¼ cup crumbled cooked bacon or imitation bacon
¼ teaspoon lemon juice
2 lettuce leaves
4 tomato slices

1. Slit the tops of the baked potatoes; leaving approximately ⅛ inch of potato pulp in the shells, remove the rest, being careful not to tear the shells. Place the potato pulp in the refrigerator for use at another meal (see Helpful Hints chapter). Flatten the shells to form "pockets."

2. Toast the sunflower seeds in a 350°F. oven for 8 to 10 minutes, or until golden brown. Watch them carefully as they burn easily. Set aside.

3. Combine the chicken, sprouts, cottage cheese, red and green bell peppers, radishes, bacon, toasted sunflower seeds and lemon juice, and mix thoroughly. Chill.

4. Line the potato pockets with the lettuce leaves. Spoon the mixture into the pockets, interspersed with tomato slices.

MEAT STUFFED SPUDS

Meat and potatoes have long been considered the staple American diet by many people. Meat stuffed spuds help to make this concept easier, less expensive and more fun. Whether you are planning a backyard picnic with Tex-Mex Chili Spuds or Sloppy Joe Spuds; a Sunday brunch with Spuds Benedict or Green Eggs and Ham in Spuds; or a St. Patrick's Day party with either Corned Beef and Cabbage Spuds or Irish Tacos, you will delight your guests and save yourself time and money.

Beef Hash in a Spud

2 baked potatoes
1 tablespoon corn oil
¼ cup chopped onion
2 tablespoons chopped parsley
1 cup coarsely ground beef
1 tablespoon Worcestershire sauce
⅓ cup milk
¼ teaspoon salt
⅛ teaspoon freshly ground black pepper
Chopped parsley for garnish

1. Cut a thin slice from the top of each potato. Remove the pulp from the potatoes, being careful not to tear the shells. Place the potato pulp in a saucepan and mash; cover and set aside. Keep the shells warm.

2. Heat the corn oil in a skillet. Add the onion and parsley and cook over low heat until tender, about 10 minutes.

3. Add the ground beef and Worcestershire sauce and cook until the beef is just barely pink. While the beef is cooking, stir the milk into the mashed potato. Add the salt and pepper and mix well. Add the potato mixture to the beef mixture and continue to cook until thoroughly heated, mixing well.

4. Heap the mixture into the warm potato shells and garnish with chopped parsley.

New England Stuffed Spud

2 baked potatoes
¾ cup Beef Stock (see Index)
1 bay leaf
¼ cup chopped onion
¼ cup finely chopped carrot
¼ cup finely chopped celery
¼ teaspoon salt
¼ teaspoon freshly ground black pepper
½ cup shredded cabbage
¾ cup chopped cooked beef brisket, or other leftover cooked beef
Snipped chives or green onion tops for garnish

1. Cut a thin slice from the top of each potato. Cool potatoes to room temperature. Remove the potato pulp, being careful not to tear the shells. Dice the potato pulp and set aside.

2. Heat the beef stock in a saucepan. Add the bay leaf, onion, carrot, celery, salt and pepper, and cook until the carrot is tender, about 10 minutes. Discard the bay leaf.

3. Add the cabbage and diced potato and mix thoroughly. Add the chopped beef and mix thoroughly.

4. Heap into the potato shells. Bake in a 350°F. oven for 15 minutes. Garnish with snipped chives or green onion tops.

Sloppy Joe Spud

2 baked potatoes
1 tablespoon corn oil
¼ cup chopped green onions
1 cup cooked ground beef round
3 tablespoons Sloppy Joe seasoning mix
1 cup tomato sauce
Dash of Tabasco (optional)
Snipped chives or green onion tops for garnish (optional)

1. Cut a thin slice from the top of each potato. Remove the pulp from the potatoes, being careful not to tear the shells. Place the potato pulp in a mixing bowl and mash; cover and set aside. Keep the shells warm.

2. Heat the corn oil in a saucepan. Add the green onions, ground beef, seasoning mix, tomato sauce and Tabasco; mix well. Cook over low heat for 10 minutes, stirring regularly. Add the mashed potatoes and mix thoroughly until the potatoes are heated through.

3. Heap the mixture into the warm potato shells and garnish with snipped chives or green onion tops.

Reuben Spud

2 baked potatoes
2 tablespoons Mayonnaise (see Index)
¼ cup milk
1 tablespoon prepared horseradish
¾ cup sauerkraut, drained
¼ cup chopped green onions
⅛ teaspoon salt
⅛ teaspoon freshly ground black pepper
1 cup small pieces of cooked corned beef
¾ cup grated Swiss or Gruyère cheese

1. Cut a thin slice from the top of each potato. Remove the pulp from the potatoes, being careful not to tear the shells. Place the potato pulp in a mixing bowl and mash; cover and set aside. Keep the shells warm.

2. Combine the mashed potato, mayonnaise and milk in a saucepan. Add the horseradish, sauerkraut, green onions, salt, pepper, corned beef and half of the cheese; mix thoroughly. Cook over low heat until the mixture is thoroughly heated.

3. Heap the mixture into the warm potato shells and sprinkle tops with the remaining grated cheese.

4. Heat in a 350°F. oven or under a broiler until the cheese has melted.

Corned Beef and Cabbage Spud

2 baked potatoes
1 tablespoon corn oil
¼ cup chopped onion
1 garlic clove, minced
3 tablespoons dry red wine
1 cup chopped corned beef
1 tablespoon spicy brown mustard
1 cup shredded cabbage, cooked crisp tender
¼ cup milk
1 teaspoon salt
¼ teaspoon freshly ground black pepper
Snipped chives or green onion tops for garnish

1. Cut a thin slice from the top of each potato. Remove the pulp from the potatoes, being careful not to tear the shells. Place the potato pulp in a mixing bowl and mash; cover and set aside. Keep the shells warm.

2. Heat the corn oil in a skillet. Add the onion and garlic and cook over low heat until tender, about 10 minutes.

3. Add the red wine, corned beef and mustard, stirring well.

4. Add the cabbage, milk, salt and pepper to the mashed potatoes and mix well. Add the potato mixture to the skillet, stirring well until heated thoroughly.

5. Heap the mixture into the warm potato shells and garnish with snipped chives or green onion tops.

Variation: Add ½ teaspoon caraway seeds in step 4.

Tex-Mex Chili Spud

2 baked potatoes
2 tablespoons corn oil
¼ cup chopped green pepper
¼ cup chopped onion
1 garlic clove, minced
¼ cup chopped jalapeño chile peppers (2 medium-size peppers)
1 cup canned chile con carne without beans
½ cup fresh tomatoes, crushed
½ teaspoon chili powder
½ teaspoon salt
¼ teaspoon freshly ground black pepper
Chopped onion for garnish

1. Cut a thin slice from the top of each potato. Remove the pulp from the potatoes, being careful not to tear the shells. Place the potato pulp in a mixing bowl and mash; cover and set aside. Keep the shells warm.

2. Heat the corn oil in a skillet. Add the green pepper, onion and garlic and cook over low heat until tender. Stir in the chile peppers, chile con carne, tomatoes and chili powder. Heat thoroughly, stirring constantly.

3. Add the mashed potatoes, salt and pepper. Stir well and heat through.

4. Heap the mixture into the warm potato shells and garnish with chopped onion.

Variation: Top each potato with 2 tablespoons of grated sharp Cheddar cheese in place of the chopped onion garnish, and place under the broiler or in the oven until the cheese has melted.

Potato Lasagna

2 baked potatoes
1 tablespoon corn oil
1 medium-size onion, finely chopped
½ cup ground beef
¼ cup dry red wine
¼ cup tomato sauce
1 small tomato, peeled and chopped, or ½ cup chopped canned
    tomato
¼ teaspoon dried basil, crushed in a mortar with a pestle
¼ teaspoon orégano, crushed in a mortar with a pestle
1 teaspoon salt
⅛ teaspoon freshly ground black pepper
½ cup grated mozzarella or Monterey Jack cheese
¼ cup sliced ripe olives
Tabasco (optional)
Chopped parsley

1. Cut a thin slice from the top of each potato. Remove the pulp from the potatoes, being careful not to tear the shells. Place the potato pulp in a mixing bowl and mash; cover and set aside. Keep the shells warm.

2. Heat the corn oil in a skillet. Add the onion and cook over low heat until tender, about 10 minutes.

3. Add the ground beef, red wine, tomato sauce, tomato, basil, orégano, salt and pepper, and cook until the meat is pink, stirring frequently. Add the mashed potato pulp, mix well, and heat thoroughly. Add the mozzarella cheese and ripe olives, and Tabasco if you use it, and stir until the cheese is melted.

4. Heap the mixture into the warm potato shells and garnish with chopped parsley.

Variation: *Vegetarian Potato Lasagna:* Substitute ¼ cup beef-flavored textured vegetable protein (½ cup cooked) for the ground beef.

Irish Taco

2 baked potatoes
1 cup hot cooked ground beef
½ cup taco sauce
½ cup grated Cheddar cheese
1 cup shredded lettuce
½ cup diced tomatoes
¼ cup chopped fresh cilantro (optional)

1. Split the tops of the potatoes. Scoop the pulp from the potatoes, one at a time, and place the pulp from one of the potatoes in a plastic bag and store in the freezer to use at another time. Mash remaining potato pulp in a mixing bowl. Flatten the 2 potato shells to form "taco shells," and keep warm.

2. Add the cooked ground beef to the mashed potato and mix well. Add the taco sauce and Cheddar cheese and mix thoroughly.

3. Place the mixture into the potato shells. Top with shredded lettuce and diced tomato.

Serve with extra taco sauce and chopped fresh cilantro if available. This is truly an international approach to sandwich making!

Dried Beef in a Spud

2 baked potatoes
⅓ cup dried beef, torn into small pieces
⅔ cup White Sauce (see Index)
1 tablespoon prepared horseradish (optional)
Pinch of black pepper (optional)
Chopped parsley for garnish

1. Cut a thin slice from the top of each potato. Remove the pulp from the potatoes, being careful not to tear the shells. Place the potato pulp in a mixing bowl and mash; cover and set aside. Keep the shells warm.

2. Combine the dried beef and white sauce in a saucepan and cook over low heat, stirring constantly, until the mixture starts to boil. Add the mashed potato, horseradish and black pepper, and continue to stir until the mixture is thoroughly heated.

3. Heap the mixture into the warm potato shells. Garnish with chopped parsley.

Steak Tartare Stuffed Spud

2 baked potatoes
1 tablespoon freshly squeezed lemon juice
½ teaspoon salt
⅛ teaspoon freshly ground black pepper
1 tablespoon Worcestershire sauce
1 drop of Tabasco
3 teaspoons prepared Dijon-style mustard
½ pound freshly ground lean beef sirloin
1 tablespoon capers
2 tablespoons minced onion
2 tablespoons minced parsley
½ cup dairy sour cream
1 tomato, peeled and finely diced
2 tablespoons finely diced green bell pepper

1. Cool potatoes to room temperature. Cut into halves and remove the potato pulp; crumble and set aside. Set the shells aside.

2. Combine the lemon juice and salt and stir until the salt is completely dissolved. Add the pepper, Worcestershire sauce, Tabasco and 1 teaspoon of the mustard; mix thoroughly.

3. Put the meat in a mixing bowl and stir in the lemon-juice mixture well. Add the capers, onion and parsley and mix well. Add the crumbled potato, combine thoroughly, and heap into the 4 potato shell halves.

4. Combine the sour cream and remaining 2 teaspoons mustard. Frost the tops of the Steak Tartare Stuffed Spuds with the mustard and sour-cream mixture, as if frosting cakes. Sprinkle the tops with the chopped tomato and chopped green pepper. Refrigerate until cold before serving.

Liver and Onion Stuffed Spud

2 baked potatoes
½ pound calf's liver
1 tablespoon butter or corn-oil margarine
1 small onion, chopped
½ teaspoon salt
¼ teaspoon freshly ground black pepper
Chopped parsley for garnish

1. Cut the baked potatoes into halves. Remove the potato pulp carefully, place in a bowl, and mash. Cover, and set aside. Keep the shells warm.

2. Wash the liver and pat it dry. Cut into ½-inch cubes and set aside.

3. Heat the butter or margarine in a skillet. Add the onion and cook over low heat for about 15 minutes, or until very soft and nicely browned.

4. Add the mashed potato, salt and pepper, and cook for 5 more minutes. Remove the potato and onion mixture from the pan and set aside. *Do not wash the pan!* Add the cubed liver to the pan and cook for about 3 minutes. The liver should be slightly pink inside. Overcooking makes it tough and strong-tasting.

5. Combine the cooked liver and potato mixture and mix well. Heat thoroughly.

6. Heap into the warm potato shells. Garnish with parsley.

German Pork and Cabbage Spud

2 baked potatoes
1 tablespoon corn oil
¼ cup chopped green onions
1 cup chopped cooked pork roast
¾ cup dairy sour cream
¾ cup sweet-and-sour red cabbage (available in jars)
¼ teaspoon salt
⅛ teaspoon pepper
½ cup applesauce
Parsley sprigs for garnish

1. Cut a thin slice from the top of each potato. Remove the pulp from the potatoes, being careful not to tear the shells. Place the potato pulp in a mixing bowl and mash; cover and set aside. Keep the shells warm.

2. Heat the corn oil in a skillet. Add the chopped green onions and cook over low heat until tender but not brown.

3. Add the chopped cooked pork roast, sour cream, mashed potatoes, sweet-and-sour red cabbage, salt and pepper, and mix thoroughly. Cook until the mixture is heated through.

4. Heap the mixture into the warm potato shells. Spoon ¼ cup of applesauce over each spud. Garnish with parsley sprigs and serve immediately.

Denver Potato Omelet Stuffed Spud

2 baked potatoes
2 tablespoons butter or corn-oil margarine
¼ cup diced cooked ham
¼ cup green pepper strips
¼ cup chopped onion
⅛ teaspoon basil, crushed in a mortar with a pestle
¼ cup condensed cream of chicken soup
2 eggs, lightly beaten
⅛ teaspoon pepper
¼ cup chopped fresh tomato
Grated Swiss cheese for garnish

1. Cut the potatoes into halves. Scoop out the potato pulp, being careful not to tear the shells. Mash pulp well and set aside in a covered bowl. Keep the potato shells warm.

2. Melt the butter or margarine in a skillet. Add the diced ham, green pepper, onion and basil, and cook until the vegetables are tender.

3. Combine the soup, mashed potatoes, eggs and pepper in a bowl and mix thoroughly. Stir into the ham mixture in the skillet and cook over low heat. As the mixture begins to set, stir so the uncooked portion can flow to the bottom. Continue stirring until the eggs are set but still moist, about 5 minutes.

4. Add the tomato and mix well. Heap the mixture into the warm potato halves. Sprinkle tops with Swiss cheese. Place under the broiler until the cheese is melted.

Ham Quiche Spud

2 baked potatoes
1 tablespoon butter or corn-oil margarine
¼ cup chopped onion
½ cup dairy sour cream
2 eggs, lightly beaten
⅛ teaspoon salt
⅛ teaspoon freshly ground black pepper
¾ cup ¼-inch cubes of Swiss cheese
½ cup chopped cooked ham
Chopped parsley for garnish

1. Cut a thin slice from the top of each potato. Remove the pulp from the potatoes, being careful not to tear the shells. Place the potato pulp in a mixing bowl and mash; cover and set aside. Set the shells aside.

2. Heat the butter or margarine in a skillet. Add the onion and cook over low heat until tender, about 10 minutes. Add the sour cream, lightly beaten eggs, and the salt and pepper, stirring constantly. Add mashed potatoes and mix well. Add cubed Swiss cheese and chopped ham and mix lightly.

3. Heap the mixture into the potato shells. Bake at 350°F. for 45 minutes. Garnish with chopped parsley just before serving.

Variations: *Beef Quiche Spud:* Substitute ½ cup chopped cooked beef for the ham, and use ¾ cup cubed sharp Cheddar cheese in place of Swiss cheese.
Bacon Quiche Spud: Substitute 6 slices of bacon, cooked crisp and crumbled, for the ham. Use the Swiss cheese.

Green Eggs and Ham in Spuds

This recipe was inspired by the Dr. Seuss classic, *Green Eggs and Ham;* these potatoes serve as a perfect entrée for a children's birthday party or for more adventuresome adults.

2 baked potatoes
2 tablespoons melted butter or corn-oil margarine
2 eggs
2 tablespoons milk
2 tablespoons chopped parsley
2 tablespoons snipped chives or green onion tops
⅛ teaspoon tarragon
⅛ teaspoon salt
Pinch of white pepper
¼ cup chopped cooked ham
2 parsley sprigs for garnish

1. Cut a thin slice from the top of each potato. Remove the pulp carefully, leaving ¼ inch of potato to line the shells. Spoon the pulp into a bowl and mash thoroughly. Cover and set aside to add to the eggs later.

2. Brush the insides of the potato shells with some of the melted butter or margarine. Place on a cookie sheet in a preheated 400°F. oven and cook until browned, approximately 30 minutes.

3. Break the eggs into a bowl and beat them with a fork or wire whisk until they are frothy. Put the milk, chopped parsley, 1 tablespoon chives, tarragon, salt and pepper in a blender container and blend until smooth. Pour the green mixture into the eggs and mix thoroughly.

4. Pour remaining melted butter or margarine into a large skillet and heat well before adding the egg mixture. Add the eggs and reduce the heat; stir constantly until eggs are almost set. Then add the chopped ham and the potato and cook until the eggs are of a desired consistency. Be careful not to overcook or the eggs will become dry.

Remove eggs from the heat and spoon them into the toasted potato shells.

5. Sprinkle the tops with remaining snipped chives and garnish each serving with a parsley sprig.

Peas and Ham Spud

2 baked potatoes
1 package dehydrated green pea soup mix
¾ cup boiling water
½ cup chopped leek, white part only
1 cup chopped cooked ham
⅛ teaspoon salt
⅛ teaspoon freshly ground black pepper
Parsley sprigs for garnish, chopped

1. Cut a thin slice from the top of each potato. Remove the pulp from the potatoes, being careful not to tear the shells. Place the potato pulp in a mixing bowl and mash; cover and set aside. Keep the shells warm.

2. Combine the soup mix and boiling water in a saucepan. Add the chopped leek and cook for 5 minutes, stirring constantly.

3. Add the mashed potatoes, heat through, and stir well. Add the ham, salt and pepper.

4. Heap into the warm potato shells. Garnish with chopped parsley and serve immediately.

Ham Soufflé in Spuds

2 baked potatoes
4 tablespoons butter or corn-oil margarine
6 tablespoons milk
¼ teaspoon salt
1½ tablespoons all-purpose flour
1 teaspoon prepared mustard
1 egg yolk, lightly beaten
1 cup finely chopped cooked ham
2 egg whites

1. Cut a thin slice from the top of each potato. Remove the pulp from the potatoes, being careful not to tear the shells. Keep the shells warm.

2. Combine the potato pulp, 2 tablespoons butter or margarine, 2 tablespoons milk and the salt in a bowl, and whip. Cover and set aside.

3. Melt remaining 2 tablespoons butter or margarine in a saucepan. Add the flour, remaining 4 tablespoons milk and the mustard and cook, stirring constantly, until thickened.

4. Remove from heat. Add the beaten egg yolk and mix thoroughly. Stir in the ham.

5. Using the electric mixer, beat the egg whites until soft peaks form. Fold into the ham mixture. Fold the ham into the potato mixture and combine well.

6. Heap the mixture into the potato shells. Bake in a 375°F. oven for 25 minutes.

Deviled Ham Stuffed Spud

2 baked potatoes
1 can (4½ ounces) deviled ham
¼ cup Mayonnaise (see Index)
¼ cup sweet pickle relish

1. Cut a thin slice from the top of each potato. Remove the pulp from the potatoes, being careful not to tear the shells. Place the potato pulp in a mixing bowl and mash. Set the shells aside.

2. Add the deviled ham to the potatoes and mash thoroughly. Add the mayonnaise, pickle relish, and stir until mixed well.

3. Heap into the potato shells.

These are good served hot, warm or cold. They make excellent picnic or brown bag lunches and are also wonderful for a cool supper on a hot night.

Alpenspitz Stuffed Spud with Mushroom Sauce

My inspiration for this recipe came from Dagmar and Steven Brezzo's presentation of Alpenspitz' Potatoes with Mushrooms at the Celebrities Cook for the Cancer Center Benefit in San Diego. The only difference is that their dish was not stuffed in a spud!

2 baked potatoes
4 tablespoons butter or corn-oil margarine
1 egg yolk, lightly beaten
¼ teaspoon salt
⅛ teaspoon grated nutmeg
1 teaspoon dillweed, crushed in a mortar with a pestle
1 tablespoon minced onion
4 slices of bacon, cooked crisp, drained and crumbled
¾ cup grated sharp Cheddar cheese
2 egg whites
Mushroom Sauce:
    4 tablespoons butter or corn-oil margarine
    1 shallot, finely chopped
    2 cups sliced fresh mushrooms
    ½ teaspoon ground coriander
    ⅛ teaspoon grated nutmeg
    1 tablespoon sherry

1. Cut a thin slice from the top of each potato. Remove the pulp from the potatoes, being careful not to tear the shells. Place the potato pulp in a mixing bowl and mash. Keep the shells warm.

2. Add the butter or margarine to the mashed potatoes and mix well.

3. Combine the beaten egg yolk, salt, nutmeg, dillweed, and onion. Mix well and add to the potato. Add crumbled bacon and grated cheese and again mix well.

4. Heap the mixture into the warm potato shells. Bake in a 350°F. oven for 30 minutes.

5. Whip the egg whites until stiff but not dry and spread over the tops of the baked potatoes. Return to the 350°F. oven until the meringue is lightly browned.

6. While the potatoes are heating, make the sauce. Melt the butter or margarine and sauté the shallot until lightly browned. Add the sliced mushrooms, coriander, nutmeg and sherry, and sauté until the mushrooms are tender.

7. Serve the mushroom sauce with the Alpenspitz Stuffed Spud.

Spuds Benedict

2 baked potatoes
4 tablespoons butter or corn-oil margarine
½ teaspoon salt
4 slices of Canadian bacon, cooked
4 eggs, poached
¾ cup Hollandaise Sauce (see Index), warm
Truffle or ripe olive slices for garnish

1. This recipe requires that several items be cooking at once, so organize your time accordingly.

2. Cut the potatoes into halves. With a knife slit the edges of the potato shells at 1-inch intervals, and flatten the shells and pulp to form the 4 bases (the "muffins") for the other ingredients. Work 1 tablespoon of butter and ⅛ teaspoon of salt into each potato half. Keep warm.

3. Place 1 slice of Canadian bacon on each potato half, top with a poached egg, and then with some warm hollandaise sauce.

4. Garnish with slices of truffle or ripe olive.

Southern Turnip Stuffed Spud

2 baked potatoes
4 slices of bacon
1 medium-size onion, chopped
1 cup mashed cooked turnip
¼ teaspoon salt
¼ teaspoon freshly ground black pepper
Chopped parsley for garnish (optional)

1. Cut a thin slice from the top of each potato. Remove the pulp from the potatoes, being careful not to tear the shells. Place the potato pulp in a mixing bowl and mash; cover and set aside. Keep the shells warm.

2. Cook the bacon until crisp and remove from the skillet to drain. Add the chopped onion to the bacon drippings in the skillet and cook over low heat until tender, about 10 minutes.

3. Crumble the bacon and add to the mashed potato. Add the turnip, salt and pepper and mix well. Add to the onion in the skillet and heat thoroughly.

4. Heap into the warm potato shells. Garnish with parsley if desired.

Hot German
Potato Salad

2 baked potatoes
6 slices of bacon
¼ cup chopped green onions
¼ cup chopped green pepper
¼ teaspoon salt
⅛ teaspoon freshly ground black pepper
2 tablespoons cider vinegar
2 teaspoons pure crystalline fructose
Chopped parsley for garnish

1. Cut a thin slice from the top of each potato. Remove the pulp from the potatoes, being careful not to tear the shells. Place pulp in a mixing bowl and crumble; cover and set aside. Keep the shells warm.

2. Fry the bacon in a skillet until crisp. Drain on a paper towel and crumble. Set aside.

3. Using the same skillet, combine the green onions, green pepper, salt, pepper, vinegar, fructose and crumbled potato and heat thoroughly, stirring lightly to keep from "mashing" the potatoes.

4. Heap the mixture into the warm potato shells and garnish with chopped parsley. This can also be served cold.

BLT Stuffed Spud

(Bacon, Lettuce and Tomato)

2 baked potatoes
¼ cup Mayonnaise (see Index)
4 slices of bacon, cooked crisp and crumbled
1 large tomato, diced
1 cup finely chopped lettuce

1. Cut a very thin slice from the top of each potato. Remove the pulp from the potato, being careful not to tear the shells. Crumble the potato pulp.

2. Combine the potato with the mayonnaise. Add the crumbled bacon, tomato and lettuce. Toss thoroughly.

3. Stuff back into the potato shells.

Variation: *Vegetarian BLT Stuffed Spud:* Substitute 4 slices of imitation bacon, cooked crisp and crumbled, for the bacon.

Moussaka Stuffed Spud

2 baked potatoes
1 tablespoon olive oil
1 small onion, finely chopped
1 garlic clove, finely chopped
2 tablespoons finely chopped parsley
½ cup tomato sauce
¼ cup dry red wine
⅛ teaspoon ground mace
½ teaspoon orégano, crushed in a mortar with a pestle
½ cup White Sauce (see Index)
½ cup finely chopped cooked lamb
½ cup grated Monterey Jack cheese
¼ cup grated Parmesan cheese

1. Cut a thin slice from the top of each potato. Remove the pulp from the potatoes, being careful not to tear the shells. Place the potato pulp in a mixing bowl and mash; cover and set aside. Keep the shells warm.

2. Heat the oil in a skillet. Add the onion and garlic and cook over low heat until tender, about 10 minutes.

3. Add the parsley, tomato sauce, wine, mace and orégano. Mix well and simmer for 30 minutes, stirring occasionally.

4. Remove from the heat. Add the mashed potato, white sauce, lamb and half of both cheeses; and mix well. Heat thoroughly.

5. Heap the mixture into the warm potato shells and top each potato with 2 tablespoons of grated Monterey Jack cheese and 1 tablespoon of grated Parmesan cheese.

6. Heat in a 350°F. oven until the cheese has melted.

Variation: *Vegetarian Greek Stuffed Spud:* Omit the lamb.

Mem Sahib's Chutney Potato

"Mem Sahib" was the term used for British wives in India; this recipe is an adaptation of one of their favorite India-inspired dishes.

¼ cup chopped walnuts
2 baked potatoes
1 tablespoon corn oil
½ cup chopped green onions, including the tops
½ cup plain yogurt
1 teaspoon curry powder
¼ cup chopped chutney
1 cup cubed cooked lamb
Chopped egg, raisins, coconut, pineapple or any other classic
    condiments (optional)

1. Toast the chopped walnuts in a 350°F. oven for 8 to 10 minutes, or until golden brown. Watch them carefully as they burn easily. Set aside.

2. Cut the potatoes into halves. Scoop out the potato pulp, being careful not to tear the shells. Mash pulp well and set aside in a covered bowl. Keep potato shells warm.

3. Heat the corn oil in a skillet. Add the chopped green onions and cook over low heat until tender, about 10 minutes.

4. Combine the yogurt, curry powder, chutney, mashed potatoes, lamb and walnuts, and add to the cooked onion in the skillet. Mix well and heat to serving temperature.

5. Heap the mixture into the warm potato shells. Serve with an assortment of classic condiments if desired.

Hot Dog and Sauerkraut Spud

2 baked potatoes
2 tablespoons butter or corn-oil margarine
1 cup sauerkraut, undrained
2 hot dogs, chopped into small cubes
1 tablespoon prepared brown mustard
Chopped parsley for garnish

1. Cut a thin slice from the top of each potato. Remove the pulp from the potatoes, being careful not to tear the shells. Place the potato pulp in a mixing bowl. Keep the shells warm.

2. Add the butter or margarine to the potatoes and mash. Add the undrained sauerkraut, chopped hot dogs and mustard, and stir until the mixture is thoroughly mixed.

3. Heap the mixture into the warm potato shells. Bake in a 350°F. oven for 10 to 15 minutes, or until the desired serving temperature is reached. Sprinkle with parsley.

Variation: Add ½ teaspoon caraway seeds to the potato mixture.

Sausage and Corn Spud

2 baked potatoes
¼ cup milk
⅓ cup dairy sour cream
1 teaspoon butter or corn-oil margarine
1 cup drained whole-kernel corn
1 teaspoon chopped parsley
¼ teaspoon salt
⅛ teaspoon freshly ground black pepper
1 can (5 ounces) Vienna sausage, chopped (1 cup)
Seasoned bread crumbs for garnish
Chopped parsley for garnish (optional)

1. Cut a thin slice from the top of each potato. Remove the pulp from the potatoes, being careful not to tear the shells. Place the potato pulp in a saucepan and mash. Keep the shells warm.

2. Add the milk, sour cream and butter or margarine to the mashed potato and mix thoroughly. Cook over low heat for 5 minutes. Add the corn, parsley, salt, pepper and chopped sausage, and continue to cook, stirring lightly, until the mixture is thoroughly heated.

3. Heap into the warm potato shells and garnish with seasoned bread crumbs or chopped parsley.

Stadium Tailgate Party Spud

2 baked potatoes
1 tablespoon corn oil
½ cup chopped onion
1 cup chopped hot dogs
2 tablespoons prepared mustard
2 tablespoons sweet pickle relish
⅛ teaspoon freshly ground black pepper
¾ cup White Sauce (see Index)
Snipped chives or green onion tops for garnish

1. Cut a thin slice from the top of each potato. Remove the pulp from the potatoes, being careful not to tear the shells. Place the potato pulp in a mixing bowl and mash; cover and set aside. Keep the shells warm.

2. Heat the corn oil in a large skillet. Add the onion and cook over low heat until tender, about 10 minutes.

3. Add the chopped hot dogs and cook until heated through.

4. Combine the mustard, relish and pepper and set aside. Heat the white sauce; add the mashed potatoes and mix well. Add the mustard and relish mixture to the potato mixture and mix well. Add to the onion and hot dogs and mix well.

5. Heap the mixture into the warm potato shells and garnish with snipped chives or green onion tops.

Pack them in a thermal chest to take with you out to the ball game; if you don't have the chest, they're also good cold.

Variation: *Stadium Tailgate Party Spud with Cheese:* Sprinkle 2 tablespoons grated Cheddar cheese on top of each potato. Place under the broiler until the cheese has melted.

FRUIT & VEGETABLE STUFFED SPUDS

Fruit and vegetable stuffed spuds offer exciting combinations of tastes and textures. The addition of nuts and seeds in some of these recipes adds still more variety in texture.

These recipes are all perfect for even strict vegetarian diets. They also run the gamut in menu planning from great breakfast ideas such as the Piña Colada Spud (which is even good for dessert) to wonderfully different dinners like Chili Bowl Spuds or Lentil Stuffed Spuds. The Simple Soup Spud is indeed simple—quick, easy and inexpensive. For a more gourmet approach to soup in a spud, try the Vichyssoise in a Spud.

Creamed Vegetarian Stuffed Spud

½ cup chopped raw almonds
2 baked potatoes
2 tablespoons butter or corn-oil margarine
¼ cup chopped onion
¼ cup chopped green pepper
1 cup cooked textured chicken-flavored vegetable protein
3 tablespoons dry white wine
2 tablespoons chopped pimiento
2 tablespoons chopped parsley
½ teaspoon salt
¼ teaspoon freshly ground black pepper
1 cup White Sauce (see Index)
¼ cup milk
Pinch of paprika
Pimiento strips for garnish (optional)

1. Toast the chopped almonds in a 350°F. oven for 8 to 10 minutes, or until golden brown. Watch them carefully as they burn easily. Set aside.

2. Cut a thin slice from the top of each potato. Remove the pulp from the potatoes, being careful not to tear the shells. Place the potato pulp in a mixing bowl and mash; cover and set aside. Keep the shells warm.

3. Heat the butter or margarine in a large skillet. Add the onion and green pepper and cook over low heat until tender, about 10 minutes. Add the vegetable protein, wine, pimiento, parsley, salt and pepper, and mix well. Stir in the white sauce.

4. Add the milk to the mashed potato mixture; mix well. Add to the ingredients in the skillet and cook to serving temperature. Add the toasted almonds with the last minute of cooking.

5. Heap the mixture into the warm potato shells, sprinkle with paprika, and garnish with pimiento strips.

Chili Bowl Spud

2 baked potatoes
1 tablespoon corn oil
1 small onion, finely chopped
1 garlic clove, finely chopped
1 teaspoon chili powder
¼ teaspoon ground cuminseed
⅛ teaspoon orégano, crushed in a mortar with a pestle
¼ teaspoon salt
Pinch of freshly ground black pepper
1 large tomato, peeled and diced
½ cup cooked kidney beans
4 tablespoons grated Cheddar cheese (optional)

1. Cut a thin slice from the top of each potato. Remove the pulp from the potatoes, being careful not to tear the shells. Place the potato pulp in a mixing bowl and mash; cover and set aside. Keep the shells warm.

2. Heat the oil in a skillet. Add the onion and garlic and cook over low heat until soft, about 10 minutes. Add the chili powder, cuminseed, orégano, salt and pepper. Mix well. Add the diced tomato and mashed potato and simmer for 15 minutes. Add the cooked beans and mix well.

3. Heap the chili into the potato "bowls" and top with grated cheese if desired.

4. Heat in a 350°F. oven for 10 minutes, or until the cheese has melted.

Lentil Stuffed Spud

2 baked potatoes
2 tablespoons corn oil
¼ cup chopped onion
1 garlic clove, minced
¼ cup grated scraped carrot
2 cups canned tomatoes, drained and chopped
¼ cup chopped green bell pepper
½ teaspoon salt
¼ teaspoon freshly ground black pepper
½ teaspoon marjoram, crushed in a mortar with a pestle
1 cup cooked lentils
Chopped parsley, snipped chives or green onion tops for garnish

1. Cut a thin slice from the top of each potato. Remove the pulp from the potatoes, being careful not to tear the shells. Place the potato pulp in a mixing bowl and mash; cover and set aside.

2. Heat the oil in a skillet. Add the onion and garlic and cook over low heat until tender, about 10 minutes. Add the carrot, tomatoes, green pepper, seasoning and marjoram, and mix thoroughly. Add the lentils and potato and combine well.

3. Heap the mixture into the potato shells and place them in a baking dish. Cover, and bake at 375°F. for 1 hour. Garnish with chopped parsley, chives or green onion tops.

Variation: *Lentil Stuffed Spud au Gratin:* Sprinkle 2 tablespoons grated Monterey Jack or Cheddar cheese over the top of each potato. Place under the broiler until the cheese has melted.

Masala Dosa Stuffed Spud

(Indian Sandwich)

2 baked potatoes
1 tablespoon corn oil
1 small onion, finely chopped
1 garlic clove, minced
2 canned green chiles, drained, seeded and finely chopped
¼ teaspoon ground turmeric
¼ teaspoon ground ginger
½ teaspoon chili powder
½ teaspoon ground coriander
½ teaspoon ground cuminseed
¼ teaspoon salt
¼ cup milk
2 tablespoons finely chopped parsley

1. Cut the baked potatoes into halves. Remove the pulp from the potatoes, being careful not to tear the shells. Place potato pulp in a mixing bowl and mash; cover and set aside. Keep the shells warm.

2. Heat the oil in a skillet. Add the onion, garlic and chiles and cook over low heat until tender, about 10 minutes.

3. Add all of the spices, the salt and milk, and mix well. Add the potato and parsley, mix well, and heat through.

4. Divide the mixture evenly into the 4 potato shells. Eat like open-faced sandwiches.

The Masala Dosa Stuffed Spud is delicious served with sliced tomatoes. Add fresh fruit for dessert and you have a filling and unusual vegetarian meal.

Stuffed Spud Stroganoff

2 baked potatoes
2 tablespoons butter or corn-oil margarine
1 small onion, thinly sliced
¼ pound fresh mushrooms, sliced (1 cup slices)
½ teaspoon paprika
½ teaspoon basil, crushed in a mortar with a pestle
⅛ teaspoon grated nutmeg
½ teaspoon salt
¼ teaspoon freshly ground black pepper
2 tablespoons sherry
½ cup dairy sour cream
Chopped parsley for garnish (optional)

1. Cut a thin slice from the top of each potato. Remove the pulp from the potatoes, being careful not to tear the shells. Place the potato pulp in a mixing bowl and mash; cover and set aside. Keep the shells warm.

2. Heat the butter or margarine in a skillet. Add the onion and mushrooms and cook over low heat until tender, about 10 minutes.

3. Add the paprika, basil, nutmeg, salt, pepper, sherry and mashed potato and cook for 5 minutes. Add the sour cream and mix thoroughly. Heat through.

4. Heap the mixture into the warm potato shells and serve at once. Garnish with chopped parsley if desired.

This is a wonderful entree for a Russian vegetarian dinner.

Variations: *Stuffed Spud Beef, Chicken or Turkey Stroganoff:* Add 1 cup chopped cooked lean beef, chicken or turkey in step 3.

Guacamole Stuffed Spud

The Guacamole Stuffed Spud is another delightful surprise. Not only is it delicious and certainly different, but it reduces the calories per spoonful of avocado considerably because potatoes are so much lower in calories than avocados.

2 baked potatoes
1 large ripe avocado, peeled and seeded
1 tablespoon freshly squeezed lemon juice
2 tablespoons finely chopped onion
1 teaspoon salt
¼ teaspoon ground cuminseed
¼ teaspoon chili powder
¼ teaspoon garlic powder
1 tablespoon dairy sour cream
1 large tomato, diced
Dash of Tabasco
Chopped green onions for garnish

1. Cut a thin slice from the top of each potato. Remove the pulp from the potatoes, being careful not to tear the shells. Place the potato pulp in a mixing bowl and mash; cover and set aside.

2. Mash the avocado until there are no lumps. Add the lemon juice, onion, salt, cuminseed, chili powder, garlic powder and sour cream; mix well.

3. Add avocado mixture to the mashed potatoes and mix thoroughly. Fold in the diced tomato and Tabasco and stir lightly until thoroughly mixed.

4. Heap the mixture into the potato shells and garnish with chopped green onions. Refrigerate until ready to serve.

Picnic Potato Salad Spud

2 baked potatoes
2 tablespoons chopped onion
2 tablespoons chopped sweet pickle
1 small celery rib with leaves, finely chopped
2 tablespoons chopped pimiento
1 hard-cooked egg, chopped
⅓ cup Mayonnaise (see Index)
1 teaspoon prepared mustard
1 teaspoon cider vinegar
¼ teaspoon salt
2 pinches of freshly ground black pepper
1 tablespoon capers (optional)

1. Cool the potatoes to room temperature. Cut a thin slice from the top of each potato. Remove the pulp, being careful not to tear the shells. Set the shells aside. Dice the pulp.

2. Combine the diced potato, onion, pickle, celery, pimiento and hard-cooked egg; stir lightly, mixing well.

3. Combine the mayonnaise, mustard, vinegar, salt and pepper and mix thoroughly. Add the capers if desired.

4. Combine potato mixture and mayonnaise mixture and again mix well.

5. Heap into the potato shells. If you wish to serve this cold, place in the refrigerator and chill.

Pritikin Stuffed Spud

This potato is served occasionally as an afternoon snack at the Pritikin Longevity Center in Santa Monica.

2 baked potatoes
2 tablespoons hoop cheese, crumbled
½ cup buttermilk
1 tablespoon chopped fresh parsley
2 teaspoons low sodium Dijon-style mustard
Pinch dillweed

1. Slit (do not halve) the baked potatoes and carefully remove the pulp into a bowl. Keep the shells warm for refilling.

2. Add all other ingredients to the potato pulp and mix with an electric mixer until well blended.

3. Refill the potato shells with the mixture. Place on a baking sheet and bake at 350°F. for 30 minutes.

Buttermilk Spud

2 baked potatoes
3 tablespoons dehydrated soup greens
½ cup buttermilk
2 tablespoons Mayonnaise (see Index)
1 tablespoon powdered buttermilk salad dressing mix
Chopped parsley for garnish

1. Cut a thin slice from the top of each potato. Remove the pulp from the potatoes, being careful not to tear the shells. Place the potato pulp in a mixing bowl and mash; cover and set aside. Keep the shells warm.

2. Reconstitute the soup greens by cooking them in water to cover for 5 minutes. Drain and set aside.

3. Combine the buttermilk, mayonnaise, mashed potatoes and buttermilk salad dressing mix, and mix thoroughly. Place over low heat, stirring constantly, until heated. Add the reconstituted soup greens and mix well.

4. Heap the mixture into the warm potato shells and garnish with chopped parsley. This is good served hot or cold.

Vichyssoise in a Spud

Serving vichyssoise in a spud bowl is an imaginative presentation for an informal patio supper, and it goes well with charcoal-broiled fish, meat or poultry.

2 baked potatoes
2 tablespoons butter or corn-oil margarine
1 medium-size onion, chopped
2 leeks, white part only, chopped
1 cup Chicken Stock (see Index)
1 bay leaf
½ cup cream
½ teaspoon salt
¼ teaspoon pepper
Snipped chives or green onion tops for garnish

1. Cut a thin slice from the top of each potato. Remove the pulp from the potatoes, being careful not to tear the shells. Place the potato pulp in a mixing bowl and mash; cover and set aside.

2. Heat the butter or margarine in a skillet. Add the chopped onion and leeks and sauté for about 3 minutes.

3. Add the mashed potatoes, chicken stock and bay leaf and mix thoroughly. Simmer the mixture, covered, for 15 minutes, or until the vegetables are tender. Remove the bay leaf and discard.

4. Whirl the mixture in a blender or push it through a fine sieve to reduce it to a velvety smoothness. Add the cream, salt and pepper and mix thoroughly.

5. Place the potato shells on the plates on which they will be served and pour the mixture into them. Refrigerate until cold. Garnish with snipped chives or green onion tops just prior to serving.

Borscht Spud

2 baked potatoes
½ cup dairy sour cream
1 can (8 ounces) beets, drained
1 teaspoon fresh lemon juice
⅛ teaspoon onion salt
⅛ teaspoon freshly ground black pepper
Sour cream for garnish

1. Cut a thin slice from the top of each potato. Remove the pulp from the potatoes, being careful not to tear the shells. Place the potato pulp in a mixing bowl and mash; cover and set aside. Set the shells aside.

2. Combine the sour cream, drained beets, lemon juice, onion salt and pepper in a blender container and blend until smooth.

3. Pour the puréed beet mixture into the mashed potatoes and mix thoroughly. Spoon into the potato shells and garnish with a dollop of sour cream.

Borscht Spuds are good served hot or cold.

Simple Soup Spud

2 baked potatoes
½ cup heated leftover soup (any kind)

1. Cut a thin slice from the top of each potato. Remove the pulp from the potatoes, being careful not to tear the shells. Place pulp in a mixing bowl.

2. Add the heated leftover soup to the potato pulp and mix lightly. Spoon mixture into the potato shells.

This is also good served cold.

G t-Well Chick n Soup in a Spud

1 baked potato
¼ cup heated Chicken Stock (see Index)

1. Cut a thin slice from the top of the potato. Using a spoon, break up the pulp in the potato. Pour the hot chicken stock evenly over the potato.

2. Serve to the patient immediately!

Peanut Butter and Jelly Spud

This is a fine after-school snack for hungry students. The potatoes are also a delicious and unusual breakfast. Serve hot or cold, depending upon the weather!

2 baked potatoes
¼ cup milk
¾ cup peanut butter
½ cup grape jelly (or your favorite kind)

1. Cut the potatoes into halves. Remove the pulp from the potatoes, being careful not to tear the shells. Place the potato pulp and milk in a mixing bowl and whip until smooth. Set the shells aside.

2. Combine the potato, peanut butter and jelly and fold, leaving streaks of peanut butter and jelly through the mixture.

3. Heap into the potato shells and garnish each with a dollop of jelly.

125

Banana and Peanut-Butter Snack Spud

2 baked potatoes
½ cup peanut butter
2 small bananas, mashed
¼ cup milk
¼ teaspoon grated nutmeg or ground cinnamon
Nutmeg for garnish

1. Cut the baked potatoes into halves. Remove the pulp from the potatoes, being careful not to tear the shells. Place the potato pulp in a mixing bowl and mash.

2. Combine the peanut butter, mashed bananas, milk and spice and add to the mashed potato. Mix with an electric mixer until very smooth.

3. Spoon the mixture into the potato shells and refrigerate for after-school snacks. Sprinkle with a little nutmeg before serving.

Vegetarian Spud

2 baked potatoes
½ cup sliced mushrooms
2 tablespoons butter or corn-oil margarine
¼ teaspoon ground ginger
⅛ teaspoon grated nutmeg
¼ teaspoon salt (celery salt optional)
⅛ teaspoon freshly ground black pepper
1 cup assorted chopped leftover cooked vegetables
¼ cup diced raw apple
½ cup dairy sour cream
Chopped parsley for garnish

1. Cut a thin slice from the top of each potato. Remove the pulp from the potatoes, being careful not to tear the shells. Place the potato pulp in a mixing bowl and mash; cover and set aside. Keep the shells warm.

2. Sauté the sliced mushrooms in the butter or margarine for about 5 minutes. Add the ginger, nutmeg, salt and pepper and mix well. Add the vegetables and the raw apple; stir well.

3. Add the sour cream to the mashed potatoes and mix thoroughly. Add to the vegetable mixture and continue to heat, stirring constantly, until thoroughly heated.

4. Heap the mixture into the warm potato shells. Garnish with chopped parsley.

Piña Colada Spud

This recipe was inspired by the famous drink of the Islands and is just as habit-forming! The Piña Colada Spud is excellent as a light luncheon entree served with cold poached fish or chicken. It also makes an unusual and nutritious dessert.

1 can (8¼ ounces) pineapple chunks
2 baked potatoes
½ cup cream or milk
2 teaspoons pineapple juice from the can of pineapple
1¼ teaspoons vanilla extract
1 teaspoon coconut extract
1 tablespoon pure crystalline fructose
Cinnamon for garnish

1. Drain the juice from pineapple chunks and reserve at least 2 teaspoons of the juice for later use in the recipe. Set pineapple aside.

2. Cut the potatoes into halves. Allow to cool to room temperature. Remove the pulp from the potato halves carefully. Place in a bowl and mash.

3. Add the cream or milk and reserved pineapple juice to the mashed potatoes and mix well until a smooth consistency is attained.

4. Add the vanilla, coconut extract and fructose to the potato mixture. Fold in the pineapple chunks.

5. Heap the mixture into the potato halves. Garnish with cinnamon.

Mincemeat Stuffed Spud

This unusual stuffed spud is delicious served with a fresh fruit and cottage cheese salad in place of a sweet roll or Danish pastry. During the holidays serve this spud with sliced turkey and scrambled eggs for brunch. Garnish the plate with a few cranberries for color.

2 baked potatoes
2 tablespoons butter or corn-oil margarine
½ cup cream or milk
1 box (9 ounces) condensed mincemeat
Ground cinnamon for garnish
Cinnamon sticks for garnish (optional)

1. Cut the potatoes into halves. Remove the pulp from the potatoes, being careful not to tear the shells. Add the butter or margarine to the potato pulp and mash. Set the shells aside.

2. Add the cream or milk, a little at a time, to the potatoes, mashing to a creamy consistency.

3. Crumble the mincemeat and add it to the potato mixture. Mix thoroughly.

4. Heap filling into the potato shells. Sprinkle lightly with ground cinnamon and garnish with pieces of cinnamon sticks if desired.

INDEX

130

131

Maria the Virgin Witch volume 2 is a work of fiction. Names, characters, places, and incidents are the products of the author's imagination or are used fictitiously. Any resemblance to actual events, locales, or persons, living or dead, is entirely coincidental.

A Kodansha Comics Trade Paperback Original.

Maria the Virgin Witch volume 2 copyright © 2011 Masayuki Ishikawa
English translation copyright © 2015 Masayuki Ishikawa

All rights reserved.

Published in the United States by Kodansha Comics,
an imprint of Kodansha USA Publishing, LLC, New York.

Publication rights for this English edition arranged through Kodansha Ltd.,
Tokyo.

First published in Japan in 2011 by Kodansha Ltd., Tokyo, as *Jyunketsu
no Maria* volume 2.

ISBN 978-1-63236-081-6

Printed in the United States of America.

www.kodanshacomics.com

9 8 7 6 5 4 3 2 1

Translator: Stephen Paul
Lettering: Evan Hayden
Editing: Ajani Oloye

Sorcière de gré, pucelle de force, page 1
French for "Witch by Choice, Maiden by Force." Pucelle means maiden, but La Pucelle (d'Orleans) was also the nickname of Joan of Arc (aka Jeanne d'Arc).

Chevauchée, page 23
A medieval form of "scorched earth" tactics that attempted to do as much damage as possible to enemy territory by riding forth with mounted troops in a lightning strike, burning and pillaging farmland and towns as they went. Though it was considered to be a mercenary's tactic, it was also used quite often by royal forces, and extensively so during the Hundred Years' War, especially by the "Black Prince," Prince Edward of Woodstock. The epithet may have come from his reputation for brutal tactics toward the French during the war.

Chevalier, page 33
The French form of the word "cavalier": a knight.

Beaufort, page 46
Referring to Henry Beaufort, the Bishop of Winchester from 1404 until his death in 1447. Beaufort was an extremely powerful and influential figure within the government of England during this time, and was actually related to the English royalty as a member of the Plantagenet line, making him a target of criticism for holding powerful positions in both church and state.

Arthur de Richemont, page 63
Also known as Arthur III, the Duke of Brittany, a feudal duchy along the northwest coast of modern-day France. He was a notable military figure during the Hundred Years' War who ultimately helped bring the conflict to a close by winning some of the final battles that drove the English from France.

Leviathan, page 95
An enormous sea monster as originally described in the Old Testament. It has been depicted in many ways since, such as a giant sea serpent or a whale (as in Moby-Dick), in countless books, comics, video games, and so on.

Golgotha, page 96
The hill outside of Jerusalem where Jesus was crucified in the Bible.

◄1► A mighty wind and huge cloud came from the north, surrounded by shining light, and blowing fire.

◄2► Something was shining like brass within the fire.

◄3► Within that were human-shaped beings that glowed with four wings, four faces, and feet like calves.

◄4► Within those beings was a fire like burning coal that also shot lightning.

◄5► Beside the beings were wheels, arranged in a way to form wheels within wheels.

In particular, the descriptions in steps one and two seem to match what occurred in the story.

If this is what the mercenaries and Maria saw, then we can find an analogy for this in the last verse of this vision in Ezekiel. In other words:

"This was the appearance of the likeness of the glory of Jehovah."

But what about steps three through five? It is a very mysterious and indecipherable description.

Some claim that this is actually a depiction of an alien or UFO encounter. Apparently, the phrase "wheels within wheels" came to refer to any phenomenon that was mysterious or inscrutable.

Raphael produced a painting called *Ezekiel's Vision*. It is indeed fashioned after the description that appears in the Book of Ezekiel. This is Raphael's interpretation of the scene, and it might prove enlightening to anyone interested.

Pardon me? "What's the point?"
How should I know that?!

At any rate, the one thing we know for certain is that the sight was so astonishing and confounding that everyone present, including me, fell unconscious. Whether it was the glory of the Lord, or the advent of some gigantic spaceship, God only knows.

Hello, I am Ezekiel.

In a scene in Chapter 8, "Virgin Witch and Angel's Servant," the group of mercenaries who attempted to desecrate me were shocked by a stunning vision. Maria and her owls, who were content to sit back and watch my plight unfold, also witnessed this scene.

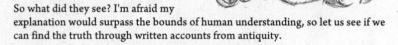

So what did they see? I'm afraid my explanation would surpass the bounds of human understanding, so let us see if we can find the truth through written accounts from antiquity.

Michael gave me my name from the prophet Ezekiel, the namesake of the Book of Ezekiel in the Old Testament. The following passage appears at the beginning of this book:

> And I looked, and, behold, a whirlwind came out of the north, a great cloud, and a fire infolding itself, and a brightness was about it, and out of the midst thereof as it were glowing metal, out of the midst of the fire. Also out of the midst thereof came the likeness of four living creatures. And this was their appearance; they had the likeness of a man. And every one had four faces, and every one had four wings. And their feet were straight feet; and the sole of their feet was like the sole of a calf's foot: and they sparkled like the colour of burnished brass. [...] As for the likeness of the living creatures, their appearance was like burning coals of fire, and like the appearance of lamps: it went up and down among the living creatures; and the fire was bright, and out of the fire went forth lightning. And the living creatures ran and returned as the appearance of a flash of lightning. Now as I beheld the living creatures, behold one wheel upon the earth by the living creatures. [...] And they four had one likeness: and their appearance and their work was as it were a wheel in the middle of a wheel.

The Book of Ezekiel begins abruptly with a description of a vision by Ezekiel the prophet, which ends just as abruptly. There is virtually no lead-in or background, leaving the passage quite mysterious.

Let us put aside the interpretations that "Ezekiel the prophet got a little too excited (ha ha)," or "The worldly church edited the original passage down to this form," and simply examine the text as it is given.

❧ *Fin*